Loving the Self-Absorbed

How to Create a More Satisfying Relationship with a Narcissistic Partner

Nina W. Brown, Ed.D., LPC, NCC

New Harbinger Publications, Inc.

Distributed in Canada by Raincoast Books

Copyright © 2003 by Nina W. Brown
      New Harbinger Publications, Inc.
      5674 Shattuck Avenue
      Oakland, CA 94609

Cover design by Amy Shoup
Edited by Wendy Millstine
Text design by Tracy Marie Carlson

ISBN-10 1-57224-354-6
ISBN-13 978-1-57224-354-5

New Harbinger Publications' website address: www.newharbinger.com

09 08 07

15 14 13 12 11 10 9 8

This book is dedicated to three of the loves in my life: Toni, Mike, and Linda.

Contents

Acknowledgments

This book could not have been written without assistance from a number of people and I want to express my appreciation to them. Catharine Sutker, the acquisitions editor, for asking me to write a book on this topic. Wendy Millstine, the hardworking copy editor at New Harbinger, who helped put the book in final form. Joan Medway, George Max Saiger, and Mary Duluy are some of my friends from the Mid-Atlantic Group Psychotherapy Society who are supportive. Sandi Lewis, Radha Horton-Parker, Chris Lovell, Bill Drewry, and Jim Cross, my colleagues at Old Dominion University who encouraged me to write on the topic. My husband, Wilford, deserves special appreciation as he helps in more ways than you can imagine. Thanks very much to all.

Chapter 1

Are You in a Relationship with a Destructive Narcissist?

Loving a self-absorbed person is hard work, as your needs and desires most often have to take second place or are ignored. This can be especially frustrating and demoralizing when you want desperately to have a mutually satisfying relationship and nothing has worked to this point. You also see your partner's positive attributes and try to minimize his or her negative and destructive behavior and attitudes for the sake of the relationship.

If this description fits your partner and your relationship, you will find some helpful suggestions in this book. It is intended to guide you in learning ways to cope with your partner and to be more satisfied with yourself.

The following are two real and personal accounts from people who describe their experiences with a self-absorbed partner.

Carol: I purchased *The Destructive Narcissistic Pattern* (Brown 1998) about a year ago. Prior to that, I had lived in a very unhappy marriage, characterized by verbal and emotional abuse. We have been in and out of counseling, but nothing seemed to help. For so many years, I struggled with what I could say or do differently to make my husband understand how his behavior was affecting me and others. This book opened my eyes.

Mike: When I first met my wife, I remember thinking that she was a little narcissistic. Unfortunately, I did not understand all that implied. She was charming, and intelligent, and we shared lots of interests and values. I really didn't care if she was somewhat self-congratulatory.

After we were married six months, we started to have relationship problems. She kept pointing out my faults, and I admit that some were real. So, I kept trying to improve. But if I did manage to improve, it seemed the standard would be raised. She treated small mistakes, like being one minute late, as betrayal, and commented that she could never trust me again. When I tried to tell her how I felt, I was told, "I don't want to hear all that negativity."

Hearing about relationships, such as the above, helped me realize that being in a relationship with someone who has a Destructive Narcissistic Pattern (DNP) is very demoralizing, shaming, and frustrating. It can produce a feeling of profound helplessness, and partners can be left without hope of ever feeling any other way. This book is an attempt to provide information for better understanding your partner as well as suggestions that may be helpful to the long-term success of your relationship.

Before we go further with explanations and descriptions, it would be helpful to determine if you are in a relationship with a destructive narcissist.

Table 1: Destructive Narcissist Rating Scale

Directions: Based on your partner, answer each of the following items using the scale.	
5—Always or almost always does this 4—Frequently does this 3—Does this sometimes 2—Seldom does this 1—Never or almost never does this	
1. Constantly looks to you to meet their needs	
2. Expects you to know what your partner expects, desires, and needs without having to ask for it	
3. Gets upset when you are perceived to be critical or blaming	

4. Expects you to put their needs before your own	
5. Seeks attention in indirect ways	
6. Expects you to openly admire them	
7. Acts childish (for example, sulks and pouts)	
8. Accuses you of being insensitive and uncaring about them without cause or notice	
9. Finds fault with your friends	
10. Becomes angry when challenged or confronted	
11. Does not seem to recognize your feelings	
12. Uses your disclosures to criticize, blame, and discount you	
13. Is controlling	
14. Lies, distorts, and misleads	
15. Is competitive, and uses any means to get what is wanted	
16. Has a superior attitude	
17. Is contemptuous of you and of others	
18. Is arrogant	
19. Is envious of others	
20. Demeans and devalues you	
21. Is self-centered and self-absorbed	
22. Has to be the center of attention	
23. Manipulates others to win admiration	
24. Is impulsive and reckless	
25. Boasts and brags	

26. Is insensitive to your needs	
27. Makes fun of others' mistakes or faults	
28. Engages in seductive behavior	
29. Is vengeful, and seeks to get even	
30. Expects favors, but does not return them	
Total	_____

Scoring

Scores will range from 30–150. Add your ratings and use the following as a guide to determine if you are in a relationship with a destructive narcissist.

126–150 **Severe**   It's likely that you are in a relationship with a destructive narcissist.

102–125 **Serious**   Your partner has many destructive narcissistic characteristics.

78–101 **Mild**   Your partner has some troubling destructive narcissistic characteristics.

54–77 **Scant**   Your partner has some underdeveloped narcissism, but few destructive narcissistic characteristics.

30–53 **No problem**   It is unlikely that you are in a relationship with a destructive narcissist.

Severe Ratings

Ratings between 126 and 150 mean that you consider your partner to have considerable behaviors and attitudes reflective of a DNP. These behaviors and attitudes have had a serious negative impact on the relationship, your self-confidence, and your self-esteem.

Serious Ratings

Ratings between 102 and 125 indicate that you perceive your partner as having many of the described destructive narcissistic behaviors. You are troubled by your partner's behavior and attitudes, especially those that diminish, devalue, and demean you. Your challenges or confrontations with your partner have not produced the desired changes, and you always seem to end up feeling worse than before you challenged them.

Mild Ratings

Ratings between 78 and 101 suggest that you perceive your partner as having some behaviors and attitudes reflective of the DNP. You have a vague discomfort with these behaviors and attitudes, but may not be able to adequately identify what is being done, said, or conveyed that causes you concern.

Scant Ratings

Ratings between 54 and 77 indicate that your partner displays some troubling behaviors and attitudes reflective of a destructive narcissist, but that these are few in number, and/or low in intensity. There may be some areas of underdeveloped narcissism, but the difficulties you may be experiencing very likely have other explanations. The underdeveloped narcissism just adds to whatever else may be present.

No Problem

If your total ratings fell below 53, your partner does not have a Destructive Narcissistic Pattern. The difficulties you experience may have other sources, and what is presented in this book is not designed to address these; however, the exercises and discussion in chapter 9 could be helpful for your personal development.

Additional Information from the Scale

The items on the scale are clustered into the types of Destructive Narcissistic Patterns that are discussed in chapters 5–8. You can get a preliminary reading for your partner by looking at the number of items that you rated above 3 for each of the designated clusters.

Type	Item group	Your Ratings 3+
Hungry	1–7	_____
Suspicious	8–13	_____
Manipulative	14–20	_____
Exhibitionist	22–30	_____

Note: Item 21 is omitted as it is reflective of all types.

You may find that there is not a strong rating for a particular category or that there are strong ratings for more than one category. However, high ratings overall can suggest that there may be some destructive narcissism. It could be helpful for you to explore all types for a better understanding of your partner, the relationship, and yourself, as well as equipping yourself with coping strategies. Indeed, many readers will see reflections for their situations in all types, but one may be dominant.

Overview of the Destructive Narcissistic Pattern

The DNP is considered to be a cluster of behaviors and attitudes similar to those thought to form pathological narcissism, as characterized by the Narcissistic Personality Disorder, which is a diagnosed condition. However, the behaviors and attitudes for the DNP are fewer and less intense or severe, and this is not a formally diagnosed condition. It is a description of behaviors and attitudes that are destructive to relationships. What follows is a brief discussion about the characteristics of the DNP, an appropriate self-focus, and some possible causes.

The concept of narcissism was named for Narcissus, a mythological character. Narcissus was a physically handsome youth who was an object of desire of the nymphs. One nymph in particular, Echo, was very attracted to Narcissus; but when she expressed her love for him, he very abruptly rejected her. She was so shamed and humiliated that she faded away until only her voice was left. The gods decided to punish Narcissus and caused him to fall in love with his reflected image in a pond. Every time he reached out to embrace the image, it would fragment and fade away. He was desolate, but could not stop looking at himself in the pond and loving the image. He pined away until only a flower remained. Many of the characteristics of destructive narcissism are present in the story of Narcissus: arrogance, self-absorption, grandiosity, lack of empathy, poorly differentiated self and object boundaries, and absence of enduring relationships.

The following discussion has certain assumptions and foundations.

1. Some of the described behaviors and attitudes are expected and appropriate for children and adolescents, but not for adults. This is what is known as age-appropriate narcissism. This book focuses on adults who display behaviors and attitudes expected or appropriate for children and adolescents.

2. There is a difference between self-absorption and self-care.

3. People with a DNP remain unaware that they exhibit behaviors and attitudes that are distressing to others.

4. People who have a DNP exhibit the troubling behaviors in different ways. Some people may have some, but not all, of the characteristics. These will also differ in intensity for each person.

5. You are encouraged to engage in self-examination to determine if and when you exhibit behaviors and attitudes more suitable for children and adolescents—just as destructive narcissists cannot see their age-inappropriate narcissism, you do not see yours.

6. Nothing you do or say will cause the other person to change. You can only change your expectations, behaviors, and attitudes, and gain more understanding of yourself and your partner.

How Your Situation Developed

You've probably given some thought to how your relationship with your partner came to be as it is today, but still cannot understand how or when it changed. It would not be unusual to find that the relationship developed in the following way. There are four phases in this description and they tend to overlap and blend into each other, making it difficult to recognize a transition until it is complete. The four phases are termed:

- connection,

- engagement,

- disillusion, and

- mired/impasse.

Phase 1—Connection

This phase marks the beginning of the relationship. You become aware of this person's existence and presence and are attracted to them. This awareness may be at a distance, or you may be introduced and begin to interact. However it starts, you feel a connection that you want to continue. You like what you see and experience, you want to get close to the person, and you want this person to be as attracted to you as you are to them. You make an effort to get information about the person in the desire to become closer.

Phase 2—Engagement

This phase is characterized by this person's seemingly total involvement with you. The person seems captivated and pleased by you, spends a considerable amount of time with you, makes an effort to try to please you, listens intently to you, and seems committed to the relationship. You thrive on the flattery, attention, and intensity. It is a wonderful feeling to have someone so interested and involved with you. It is in this phase that you most likely gave yourself over to the relationship. For example, you married the person.

Phase 3—Disillusion

You gradually became aware of this phase. You may have denied or suppressed awareness of what was happening for a long time. What probably happened was that your partner began to be less captivated, interested, and enchanted with you. Your partner began to criticize, blame, and devalue you at times, but these events were interspersed with the behaviors you liked so much in Phase 2. You probably discounted the uncomfortable behaviors, shrugged them off, or explained them away. You also tried to change in an effort to please your partner, and that seemed to work for a while. You redoubled your efforts to get back to the feelings and quality of the relationship you experienced in Phase 2, but were unsuccessful. The withdrawal of interest and critical comments were very painful for you, and you accepted the blame and fault for your partner's feelings and the impact on the relationship.

Phase 4—Mired/Impasse

In spite of all your self-examination, attempts to change, sacrifices of your self-interest and self-worth, and efforts to please your partner, the desired return to Phase 2 of the relationship did not happen. You became aware (hopefully) that your efforts were to no avail. Your partner became even more dismissive, devaluing, uninterested, and critical of you. If you are like many people, you kept redoubling your efforts, continuing to do what did not work before and is not working now. What you do not want to accept is that what you are doing to recapture their interest is never going to work. Your efforts did not, are not, and will not get you what you want.

If you are reading this book, you are most likely in or at the end of Phase 4. Before continuing, let's do an exercise to increase your awareness of the emotional roller coaster you've been on for some time, and anchor you in the present.

Grounding Exercise 1:
My Roller Coaster of Feelings

Materials: Five sheets of paper, one for writing and four for drawing. A pen or pencil and a variety of crayons or felt markers.

Directions: Sit in silence, close your eyes, and reflect on your course of the relationship with your partner.

1. Start with Phase 1—Connection. When you think you remember all the feelings you experienced in Phase 1, open your eyes, make a list of these feelings, and label them Phase 1.

2. Close your eyes and recapture the feelings from Phase 2—Engagement. Make a list of these feelings with the label Phase 2.

3. Close your eyes, and remember the feelings from Phase 3, though it may be unsettling. Make a list of these.

4. Do the same for Phase 4—Mired/Impasse. These are your present feelings about your partner and the relationship. Make a list of these and label them Phase 4.

5. Select two to three colors to represent the feelings for each phase. You will have eight to twelve different colors. Even though you may have more than two to three feelings for the phase, select colors that represent the overall collection of feelings and those that are most intense.

6. Label the remaining sheets of paper Phases 1–4.

7. Use the colors you selected for each phase to draw lines, shapes, or any representation that reflects the highs and lows of the feelings experienced for the particular phase. For example, you may have selected red, green, and purple for Phase 1 feelings of excitement, hope, and attraction.

When you are finished, look at what you've written and drawn. This will give you a better awareness of what you experienced in the past as well as what you are experiencing today. Some feelings you may be experiencing at present include:

- worthlessness,
- inadequacy,
- ineffectualness,
- devaluation,
- impotency,
- rejection,
- uneasiness or not knowing what to expect,
- helplessness,
- boredom,
- frustration,
- deadening of emotions,
- incompetency,
- anger,
- loneliness,
- abandonment, and
- self-blaming.

It might make you feel slightly better to know that most of these are the same feelings that experienced therapists feel when working with narcissists. They too go through a version of the same phases with this type of client, where the therapeutic relationship generally begins with the narcissist idealizing the therapist, then moving to where the therapist is not adequate, only gradually leading to the realization that the therapeutic gains are scant or non-existent. Along the way, the therapist can begin to have many of the negative feelings described above. Even experienced people often cannot recognize a narcissist at first, and are well into therapy before recognition sets in. Their emotional involvement with the client differs in kind from your emotional involvement with your partner, but is very similar in intensity.

Knowing that others experience narcissists in ways similar to the way you experience your partner can give you some comfort. You are not alone with your experience and feelings. However, this comfort is not sufficient to help you:

- understand the behaviors and attitudes of your partner,

- institute protective and coping strategies, and

- become more aware of how your attitudes, irrational assumptions, and other acts help your partner continue to have a negative impact on you.

These are the major topics explored in the remaining chapters.

An Additional Assumption

There is one more assumption that needs to be stated. That is, you have decided to remain in a relationship with a person who has a DNP. Your reasons for persisting are personal; each person may have very different reasons, and your reasons are not a part of the material presented in this book. They are simply accepted as unique and valid for you. This book focuses on understanding your partner and yourself and exploring protective and coping strategies.

Not addressed in this book is the relationship itself, as each relationship is different and complex. You will not find strategies and suggestions for improving or changing the relationship. That is beyond the scope of this book.

The material is not designed to help you effect changes in your partner. This cannot be overemphasized, as it is likely that you have a yearning, need, and fantasy to have your partner change. It isn't that your partner cannot change. I am convinced that they too are capable of developing age-appropriate narcissism. However, it is an individual and personal decision for that person. In all likelihood, it is impossible for you to change your partner. The only person you can change is yourself. Deciding to remain in the relationship can mean that you will have to make significant changes in your behaviors and attitudes. A better understanding of your partner and yourself can guide you in making these changes.

Definition of Terms

There are some terms and concepts that are used in this book that are important for your understanding of the material, and many of them may be unfamiliar. These terms and concepts come from the professional literature in psychology and counseling. What follows are brief descriptions for these terms and concepts as used in this book. Readers who want more in-depth descriptions are encouraged to refer to the literature on object relations and self-psychology.

The terms and concepts to be defined are:

- separation and individuation,

- age-appropriate narcissism,

- underdeveloped narcissism,

- projection,

- projective identification,

- emotional contagion, and

- a destructive narcissistic pattern.

Separation and Individuation

The process of perceiving oneself as apart and distinct from the mother (separation) begins when you are a toddler, according to Margaret Mahler (1968), and continues throughout life. This is a complex psychological process, and the amount of success you have at achieving separation is complicated by the way your mother perceives the process. For example, overly concerned mothers work to prevent separation. Because this is an internal and unconscious process, it is not under the conscious control of either you or your mother.

The other part of the process is called individuation. This refers to developing a sense of one's self: who you are apart from mother. This is based on the notion that infants perceive themselves as fused with, or a part of, their mother in a psychological sense. They were part of mother in a physical sense, but now consider mother as a part of them. The caretaking role of the mother supports this perception. However, a necessary developmental task is to have a self-identity that is yours alone. This too can be a life-long process, as is separation.

Age-Appropriate Narcissism

It can be helpful to understand that there is age-appropriate narcissism and that narcissism does not have to be destructive or pathological. This concept is also helpful in understanding that healthy adult narcissism takes time to develop. There are different expectations for the level and kind of self-absorbed behaviors and attitudes for children, adolescents, and adults. And there is potential for growth and development.

The concept of age-appropriate narcissism proposes that infants and children are expected to be grandiose, to have an entitlement attitude, and to have other self-absorbed behaviors and attitudes. After all, they only know or are aware of what they perceive and feel. They are conscious only of their worlds and realities. Adolescents are expected to have successfully completed some separation and individuation, to have a better understanding of personal limitations, to possess an increased awareness of others as distinct and apart from themselves, and to be well on their way to developing a self-identity. Adults are expected to be even further along in development and growth in these areas, to be better able to control their impulses, to be empathic and care for others, and to be able to be both independent and interdependent. When adults, the focus for this book, have not developed age-appropriate narcissism, they act, think, feel, and have unconscious attitudes reflective of those that are more appropriate for infants, children, and adolescents. Indeed, there can be many instances when you are dealing with an angry, frustrated baby located in an adult's body during interactions with someone who has a Destructive Narcissistic Pattern.

Underdeveloped Narcissism

The course of development is uneven for the behaviors and attitudes of narcissism, whether destructive or healthy. That is, you can be well along in development for an entitlement attitude, where you are willing to delay gratification and are able to recognize and respect the rights of others, but are not as well developed in another aspect, such as recognizing and respecting other's boundaries. It would be unusual to find an adult who has not developed from the infantile state in some ways.

A primary point about underdeveloped narcissism is that none of us are aware of or can see our personal aspects of underdevelopment. This is important to remember, because the person with a DNP absolutely cannot see what they are doing that arouses the negative feelings you experience with them. Your attempts to make the person understand how you feel about the impact of their behaviors and attitudes on you will fail, as they remain totally unaware of their underdeveloped narcissism.

The challenge, to those of us who consider ourselves more adult and developed, is to become aware of and examine our own underdeveloped narcissism. The many exercises and scales in this book have that focus and intent.

Projection

This is a common defense mechanism employed unconsciously and used to protect you from anxiety produced by unwanted thoughts and feelings. It is a way to put the discomfort on someone else, so that you don't have to feel it. The first part of the process is called *splitting*, in which the discomfort or unwanted feeling is split off from your self. It is then either *repressed*, put in your unconscious where you can stay unaware of its existence, or it is *projected* on someone else.

The second part of projection occurs when you've put this stuff on someone else, and then react to this person as if he or she felt the feeling that you did not want. For example, Mary was very angry, but she was also fearful of her anger and saw herself as never becoming angry. However, this time she was angry. She projected this anger on her friend and accused him of being angry. Her friend was not angry, but Mary continued to react to him as if he were angry.

All this happens very quickly, and on the unconscious level.

Projective Identification

This process begins with projection as described in the previous section. There is an additional step and complication. In projective identification, the person receiving the projection:

- accepts and incorporates the projection,

- identifies with some or all of the projected feeling, and

- acts on the incorporated and identified projection.

If there were a projective identification in the previous example, then Mary's friend would accept the anger, identify with it, and then become and act angry. Mary would feel relief, because she got rid of the unwanted anger, but her friend would be angry without really understanding why he was feeling that way, when he was not angry before.

You may have experienced something like this in an interaction in which you suddenly had a feeling you couldn't explain. For example, you were feeling a mild version of irritation, but it seemed to intensify during the interaction, and you were surprised at how strongly you felt. That could have been a projective identification.

The projection and the identification happen on an unconscious level, although the results are experienced on the conscious level. There is even a definition for projective identification that has the projector, such as Mary in the example, staying connected to the projected feeling, and manipulating the projection in the receiver. For example, in the illustration above, Mary's friend would be manipulated to act on the identified projection and to become angry when he was not previously angry.

The concept of projective identification is part of an explanation for why you can feel and react as you do in interactions with a destructive narcissist. If you've ever been in a interaction with a narcissist and left feeling confused, frustrated, all churned up, angry, or scared, while that person left feeling okay, then you could have been the receiver of a projection, identified with part or all of it, and then acted on it without a conscious awareness of what happened.

Emotional Contagion

In the book *Emotional Contagion,* Hatfield and her colleagues present the results of research on "catching other's feelings" (1994). The reported results support the notion of senders and receivers of emotions, and explain how the process takes place. Some of the theory is very similar to the notion of projective identification, but in addition it highlights the verbal cues, nonverbal cues, and differences in personality for senders and receivers.

Senders have many characteristics similar to those for destructive narcissists, such as:

- indifference to others,

- feeling entitled to manipulate others, and

- using nonverbal cues, such as eye contact, to manipulate and control.

Receivers have many characteristics of those people who have constant and regular contact with a destructive narcissist and are consistently frustrated and churned up after those interactions. The theme of the book is that you can "catch" emotions from other people.

A word of caution here. Catching others' emotions does not mean you are empathizing with that person. If you were empathizing, you would voluntarily open yourself to experiencing the other person's feelings, and most importantly, you would retain a sense of yourself. This means that you would not incorporate and identify with the feeling, nor would you act on and retain the feeling. If you feel that you are being empathic with a destructive narcissist, but cannot let go of the feeling or find that you are wondering about the intensity you feel, then you have not been empathic. You are experiencing projective identification and/or emotional contagion.

A Destructive Narcissistic Pattern

The concept of a Destructive Narcissistic Pattern is organized around the following points.

- People can have and exhibit age-appropriate narcissism.

- Adult narcissism can be categorized on a continuum ranging from pathological to healthy.

- There are points on the continuum to describe less than healthy adult narcissism that cannot be categorized as pathological.

- A cluster of behaviors and attitudes describe these points for less than healthy adult narcissism, and more toward healthy than pathological narcissism.

- The cluster of behaviors and attitudes closest to pathological defines the pattern of destructive narcissism.

The destructive narcissist is someone who has a set of behaviors and attitudes that are less intense and fewer in number than those that describe a pathological narcissist. Further, the pathological narcissist must be diagnosed by someone qualified to do so, and that is beyond the scope of this book.

The cluster and pattern of behaviors and attitudes considered as descriptive of destructive narcissism are described in the next chapter. In addition to those in the next chapter, other characteristics include:

- the inability to develop and maintain satisfying relationships,

- a sense of detachment or aloofness,

- a feeling of being apart and different from others,

- lack of a real and meaningful connection to others,

- a strong need to defend the self,

- a view of the world as a very dangerous place for the self,

- strong needs to have others mirror or reflect their inflated self-perception, and

- a yearning for and, at the same time, a fear or terror of intimacy.

Some Advice

Advice is always risky, as you do not know what the other person wants or needs. It's even more risky when trying to communicate via something detached, like this book. But, there are a few things that you need to take under advisement. If you are convinced, or feel reasonably certain, that you are in a relationship with a destructive narcissist, you may be tempted to do all or any of the following.

- Tell your partner that he or she is a destructive narcissist.

- Confront your partner about their behavior and attitudes.

- Leave this book where your partner can see it with the hope that they will read it and see what they are doing.

- Give your partner the book and tell them to read it, since it's about them.

Do not do any of the above, or anything similar. Here is why these acts are not helpful. Persons with a destructive narcissistic pattern cannot see the behaviors and attitudes they exhibit as you and others perceive them. They are unaware of the impact on you, and are well defended against knowing. Further, your attempts to make them aware or get through to them will fail, and will be perceived as threats to their core essential self. This will bring out their defenses for protection. The defenses are likely to be hostile, aggressive, strong, and immediately available to them, so that they are able to attack and mount a strong counteroffensive in a nano-second. You generally do not win or make any headway, and can find yourself in a worse position than before.

This book is written for you, not for the other person who may have a destructive narcissistic pattern. Use it in the intended way, and you can get some sense of what you're up against, how to fortify yourself, a guide to examining your underdeveloped narcissism, and suggestions for how to develop your own healthy adult narcissism.

Healthy Adult Narcissism

What does healthy adult narcissism encompass? What are some indicators that it has been achieved? How can you know that you have developed it or are well on your way to achieving it? Consider healthy adult narcissism to be both a realistic and an ideal goal. Realistic in the sense that you can achieve some measure of healthy adult narcissism. However, this is a lifelong process, and you may find that you need to continue to be aware and work on it throughout your life. Staying aware that you may have aspects of underdeveloped narcissism, of which you remain oblivious, is necessary.

Some of the characteristics of healthy adult narcissism include:

- creativity,

- an appropriate sense of humor,

- empathy,

- commitment to a relationship,

- the ability to form and maintain lasting and satisfying relationships,

- altruistic endeavors,

- acceptance of self and of others,

- meaning and purpose for one's life,

- aesthetic appreciation, and

- ability to delay gratification.

Strategies to promote further development for healthy adult narcissism are presented in chapter 9.

Note to readers: To reduce awkward sentence construction, and at the same time attend to gender-neutral language, I have used all masculine pronouns for chapters 3, 5, 7, and 9; and all female pronouns for chapters 2, 4, 6, and 8. Both masculine and feminine are meant when these are used.

Chapter 2

The Destructive Narcissistic Pattern

What is a Destructive Narcissistic Pattern? This chapter defines and describes the attitudes and behaviors that, when intense and clustered, are indicative of the DNP. Though these attributes are less intense and may be less numerous than those for pathological narcissism, they are sufficient to be troubling to relationships and to that person's satisfaction with their life. The behaviors and attitudes that will be discussed are:

- entitlement,
- grandiosity,
- impoverished self,
- arrogance,
- need to be unique and special,
- narrow emotions and expressions,
- lack of empathy,
- inappropriate or no sense of humor,
- emptiness at the core,
- inability to recognize or respect others' boundaries,
- tendency to be attention seeking,
- hunger for admiration

- envy, and

- expecting of favors without returning them.

Each will be presented with a short list of representative behaviors and attitudes. These are not all-inclusive, but can be used as a guide for judging if your partner meets the description. Try to stay focused on frequent and observable behavior, not your inferences. Your inferences may be correct, but it is fairer to look at behavior. It could also be helpful to review these behaviors and attitudes to identify any that may fit you. These can serve as cues to your underdeveloped narcissism.

Entitlement

An entitlement attitude can be very upsetting, as it conveys an assurance that is unwarranted. It's like a 300-pound gorilla has barged in and taken over with total disregard for anyone else. And, if challenged, the person with this attitude becomes hurt, enraged, or exhibits complete indifference, thus intensifying the distress you feel. The unconscious assumption for an entitlement attitude is that the person with the attitude has a perfect right to do or say whatever he or she desires and that no one should object. This is the person who takes unearned credit for others' work, off-loads responsibility, feels that her needs should have priority, says cutting and demeaning things to others, feels that no one should object to her behavior, is quick and eager to point out others' errors and flaws, and takes more than her fair share most of the time.

As you read the following list, think of your partner's behavior over a period of time.

Indices of Entitlement Behaviors and Attitudes

Does your partner frequently do five or more of the items in the list?

- Pushes to have her ideas, position, or opinion accepted.

- Tells you what you ought, or should, think or do.

- Insists that you wear, or not wear, the colors or styles that she likes.

- Chooses activities for you (for example, movies, sport lessons, etc.).

- Makes decisions for you or for the family without consultation.

- Solicits opinions, but guides the discussion to the decision or conclusion that she wants or feels is best.

- Expects deference due to age, wisdom, education, intelligence level, etc.

- Makes unilateral decisions about major life changes or expenditures, such as moving, buying a car, house, furniture, etc.

- Decides what social activities are acceptable.

- Insists that chores such as cleaning, yard work, house organization, etc., be done her way.

Grandiosity

An overinflated perception of self is a common definition for grandiosity, but does not begin to capture the expansiveness of the self-absorption and self-perception. The grandiose person is under the unconscious assumption that she *causes* things to happen, is omnipotent, cannot make errors or be wrong, is vastly superior to others, and can do many grand things.

Grandiose Behaviors and Attitudes

Read the following and determine if your partner frequently exhibits five or more of the described behaviors and attitudes.

- Feels that her wishes, desires, and opinions should receive preferential consideration.

- Feels that she can *make* others feel a certain way. For example, she can say something that makes someone angry.

- Feels that if something goes wrong, it usually happens because she did not get what was needed to make it go right (for example, others did not give your partner correct information or they were not clear in their communications).

- Sees or hears of the homeless or the poor and wonders why some people cannot be self-supporting or self-sufficient.

- Thinks that she knows more than most and is more intelligent or talented.

- Says that things would be better if people would just listen to her.

- Gives orders and expects prompt obedience.

- Expects others to drop what they are doing when she needs something.

- Feels that she does things right and wishes that others could be more like her.

The Impoverished Self

Embedded, repressed, and denied in grandiosity is the self that is poor, needy, and inadequate. This part of grandiosity is unknown to that person, although others may glimpse it from time to time. This impoverished self is more evident for the Hungry destructive narcissist, and may not be seen at all for the Exhibitionist destructive narcissist (these types are discussed in later chapters). The impoverished self is seen in the grandiose person's basic assumptions that others exist only to serve them, that they are entitled to call upon that service whenever it is wanted, and that others should provide it when it is needed without being told to do so—that is, others should read their minds. Does your partner do five or more of the following?

Clues to the Impoverished Self

- Feels that other people try to make her feel humiliated, embarrassed, or shamed.

- When others disagree with your partner, they are trying to show your partner as inferior or wrong.

- Will not give an opinion or information unless absolutely convinced it is correct in every way for fear of appearing stupid.

- Is alert to the possibility that others are trying to insult or put her down.

- Gets great satisfaction when she can show others as being wrong or misinformed.

- Needs someone to be on her side and gets angry when you do or say something that seem's to support the other side.

- Needs you to be in total agreement and gets upset when you differ with her.

- Feels there is something wrong with the relationship if you don't totally agree with her.

- Feels that others have to understand that your partner ought to be able to get what is wanted or needed from them.

Arrogance

Arrogance is not easily separated from entitlement and grandiosity. It is discussed separately here to emphasize how it is unconsciously exhibited in behaviors and attitudes to convey contempt and superiority.

Arrogant Behaviors and Attitudes

Does your partner do five or more of the following?

- Makes sure to associate only with people considered equal or higher in status.

- Discounts the opinions and ideas of less educated people.

- Disapproves of people who are uneducated, poor, or ignorant.

- Considers people who have not achieved as much as she had as undisciplined or as not trying hard enough.

- Seems convinced that she knows what is best for others.

- Want to be considered by others as superior in talent, intelligence, wealth, etc.

- Seems conscious of her status, achievements, wealth, and family historical status.

- Belongs to social groups, church, and other organizations because of the status these convey.

- Looks down on people who are unable to get their act together.

- Believes that people will get what they deserve, regardless of their efforts, family circumstances, and native abilities.

Unique and Special

Each person in the world is unique, and it is pleasurable to be considered special at times. However, the person with a DNP expects to be considered unique and special by everyone all of the time and gets upset when these expectations are not met. Reflect on your experience and recall some situations where your partner became upset and you were puzzled about the cause. Some situations may even have been with you. It is possible that you or others did or said something that failed to recognize your partner's uniqueness and specialness, thus leading to your partner becoming upset. It could have been a small thing, but was considered major by your partner because it did not acknowledge that she was unique and special.

Indices of Wanting to be Unique and Special

Do five or more of the following fit your partner?

- Becomes impatient when she has to wait in line (for example, at the bank).

- Gets in the express line at the grocery store with more than the maximum number of items.

- Becomes upset when she is ignored or overlooked.

- Subtly solicits flattery from others.

- Bends or breaks rules that she thinks are silly.

- Expects to receive preferential treatment.

- Asks others to do favors for her.

- Borrows things and fails to promptly return them.

- Speeds or runs red traffic lights.

- Cuts in line because she is in a hurry.

Narrow Range of Emotions

People who have a DNP tend to feel and express a narrow range of emotions. The one emotion that is experienced and expressed is anger. Anger is expressed in its many variations, such as resentment, fury, sulking, and withdrawal. This anger can be easily triggered. These people do not experience many other emotions, such as happiness, affection, annoyance, and apprehension. They may speak the words, but the feelings behind the words are missing. Read the following list of behaviors and attitudes with your partner in mind.

Experiencing and Expressing Emotions Scale

Does your partner fail to do any of the following things, or do them so infrequently that it seems as if they never happen?

- Say she is happy, content, or fulfilled.

- Tell someone she likes them.

- Express pleasure for a small delight, such as seeing an unexpected field of flowers.

- Say that she is annoyed or irritated.

- Tell someone her feelings about what they are doing or saying.

- Recognize and express when she is sad or dejected.

- Freely admit that she feels out of sorts, confused, or anxious.

- Accept her feelings rather than rationalizing or denying their validity.

- Take responsibility for her feelings, instead of thinking that others are making her feel a certain way.

- Allow her real feelings to show on her face, or openly express them.

Lack of Empathy

The person with a DNP is so self-absorbed that they cannot empathize with others. While you may have experienced your partner not being empathic with you, you probably thought that they were choosing to be unempathic. You also probably tried to be more empathic with your partner in an effort to connect and to encourage her to be empathic in return but were unsuccessful. What you did not know, or did not accept, is that your partner could not be empathic. It is not a conscious choice on your partner's part, it is an inability to empathize. Empathizing with others is a foreign concept to those with a DNP.

While it is neither suggested nor considered possible to be empathic with everyone all of the time, it is beneficial to relationships to be empathic some of the time. If you are in a relationship where you cannot expect to receive any empathy, or very little empathy, you may need to understand the impact of this lack of empathy on you and your feelings about the relationship. You may also want to understand how you are demonstrating a lack of empathy in other relationships that are important to you. Becoming more empathic with a partner who has a DNP is counterproductive and frustrating. Enhancing your empathy with others, such as your children and best friends, can be beneficial to you and to them.

Lack of Empathy Behaviors and Attitudes

Does your partner exhibit five or more of the behaviors and attitudes in the following list?

- Abruptly changes the topic in a discussion.
- Says things to try to decrease someone's emotional intensity.
- Tries to soothe people who are upset.
- Becomes distracted when listening to people.
- Becomes bored when listening to people.
- Finishes the speaker's thought or sentence (including children).
- Tells other poeple what they mean or what their motives are.

- Asks questions as a way of showing their interest.

- Wants details about others or their situations.

- Not respond to emotionally intense expressions of others.

You may think that some of these items are a show of empathy, but they are not. For example, if you think that asking questions shows interest and empathy, you are making a common mistake. Questions, by definition, are not empathic, they are a request for more information. When you are empathic, you sense or feel the other person's feeling without losing your sense of self. Thus, being empathic means that you are able to identify the other person's feelings and are able to verbalize what these are. You only ask questions for cognitive material, not feeling material. Some of these items can show sympathy, but again, that is not empathy.

No Sense of Humor

An adult with healthy narcissism has an appropriate sense of humor, appropriate in the sense that they are able to laugh at life's absurdities and at themselves. They can see the humor in silly things and laugh often. On the other hand, people with a DNP do not find anything about themselves to be humorous and are offended if anyone else does. They smile and chuckle but do not really laugh. They fail to find the humor in many situations where others can see it and have become adept at hiding their inability to see humor. What is considered to be an inappropriate sense of humor?

Inappropriate Sense of Humor Behaviors and Attitudes

Read the following list of behaviors and attitudes to see if five or more fit your partner.

- Enjoys jokes that focus on characteristics of people from different racial/ethnic/national origin groups.

- Laughs at sexist jokes.

- Thinks that someone else's discomfort or loss of dignity is funny.

- Tells sexual or erotic jokes in mixed gender company.

- Tells or laughs at gay and lesbian jokes.

- Laughs when someone receives a deserved rebuke.

- Does not find puns to be funny.

- Does not laugh out loud when they read or see something funny.

- Laughs at jokes about handicapped people.

- Refuses to laugh at themselves.

Empty

It is very difficult to explain the emptiness at the core that the destructive narcissist feels. Part of the difficulty is that the term, empty, is usually defined as the absence of something with boundaries, such as an empty cup. It is much harder to describe an inner emptiness that you can only imagine. Yet many people who come to therapy and are later found to be narcissistic have this emptiness as one of their concerns or complaints.

The best that I've been able to do for a description is to imagine being disoriented and having sensory deprivation. There is nothing available to illuminate or to provide a foundation. Imagine that you are in a place like this, where there is nothing to give a sense of security, no landmarks or other visually orienting devices, no sounds—nothing but you. Think of what it would be like to be somewhere, you don't know where, and not be able to use any of your senses to get a fix on anything. There would be no way of knowing anything and it would be terrifying. That, to me, is what emptiness at the core is like for the destructive narcissist.

This emptiness should not be confused with loneliness, alienation, or depression. In contrast, these states have considerable feelings, although most of the feelings are painful, whereas emptiness is an absence of feeling. There is also no meaning or purpose for one's existence, and the person who feels this emptiness does not know how to obtain meaning and purpose. People who are lonely, alienated, or depressed do have some understanding of how they could get meaning and purpose. The person with a destructive narcissistic pattern does not.

Clues to Emptiness at the Core

Read the following clues to see if five or more of these fit your partner.

- The extent and quality of your partner's social support system is limited and unsatisfying.

- Is constantly dissatisfied with her relationships with others, including you.

- Makes negative statements about satisfaction with the quality of her life.

- Has no, or a very limited, spiritual life.

- Cannot discuss the meaning and purpose of her life.

- Does not have reasonable and attainable personal goals.

- Cannot reach out and connect to others in meaningful ways.

- Is unaware of many parts of her life.

- Has no connections and rarely acts to benefit others outside the family.

- Cannot, or rarely, feels and expresses either joy or sadness.

Fails to Recognize Boundaries

People with a DNP fail to recognize physical and psychological boundaries. They have a flawed understanding of where they end and where others begin. They do not recognize others as unique and distinct individuals, consider others to be extensions of their self, and think, consciously and unconsciously, that they can control others.

Psychological boundaries develop as a part of the separation and individuation process that begins around the age of eighteen months and continues throughout life. People who do not begin or successfully complete age-appropriate separation and individuation fail to adequately respect other's psychological and physical boundaries. The person with a DNP often fits this description.

Lack of Recognition and Respect for Others' Boundaries Behaviors

Read the following list and determine if your partner frequently does five or more of these.

- Enters someone's room or office without knocking (including children's rooms).

- Does not wait for permission to enter someone's room or office.

- Goes through someone's drawers, desk, or personal belongings to find something she wants or needs.

- Borrows others' possessions without asking first.

- Hugs or touches someone without asking their permission.

- Accepts or rejects invitations without first checking with you.

- Makes decisions for others.

- Expects her children and partner to immediately stop what they are doing to do something that she wants them to do.

- Gives orders and expects others to obey her.

Attention Seeking

An incessant need for attention is a characteristic for many with a DNP, and these people strive for it from everyone. It's almost like being around a two-year-old child who is noisy, charming, insistent, and demanding that everyone's attention remain on them. For an adult, the goal is the same, although the means of getting attention can differ from those used by children. On the other hand, many behaviors are the same as those used by children.

Attention Seeking Behaviors

Does your partner frequently do five or more of the following?

- Talks loudly.

- Arrives late and/or leave early with much fanfare.

- Interrupts others' conversations.

- Becomes miffed when ignored.

- Tells jokes or funny stories at inappropriate times.

- Sulks or pouts.

- Says provocative things.

- Challenges others' ideas or opinions.

- Pushes to have her ideas accepted over others' ideas.

- Wears clothes that are intended to gain attention, shock, or get compliments.

Admiration Hungry

Persons with a DNP tend to be hungry for admiration and can never be filled up. They never get enough. There is no such thing as too much admiration for them, and they seek admiration from everyone all of the time. This state can also be accompanied by a hypersensitivity to any hint of criticism. This need goes way beyond wanting to be recognized and appreciated for what you are and do. It is an excessive need. Destructive narcissists, however, remain oblivious to their need and behavior.

Indications of Admiration Hungry Behaviors and Attitudes

Does your partner frequently do five or more of the following?

- Becomes profoundly disappointed when her efforts are not openly recognized or acknowledged.

- Brags and/or boasts.

- Buys things to get others to notice or pay compliments.

- Seeks awards, plaques, certificates, trophies, etc.

- Wants others to envy her.

- Makes sure that others are aware of her accomplishments.

- Inflates her accomplishments.

- Engages in self-promotion.

- Takes credit for unearned accomplishments.
- Talks about herself at every opportunity.

Envious

Envy is wanting what someone else has and feeling that they are not as deserving of it as you are. It carries the assumption that the other person is inferior in some way and that, because of your superiority, you should be favored. Many people will have moments of envy, but people who have a destructive narcissistic pattern are envious most of the time, as they tend to feel superior and entitled and are grandiose. They are convinced that they should receive praise, goods, services, promotions, awards, recognition, and anything else they desire, because they are "more worthy." These people will also denigrate and devalue others who receive the things that they consider to be rightfully theirs.

There are three aspects to envy that come into play. Envious people:

- think they are deserving and superior,
- consider others as undeserving and inferior, and
- are consumed with a desire to be envied by others for being more deserving and superior.

Wanting to be envied is an outgrowth of excessive admiration-seeking and carries a deeply ingrained sense of superiority.

Indications of Envy

Does your partner frequently do five or more of the following?

- Boasts about her possessions.
- Goes into debt to get unnecessary things to impress others.
- Takes unearned credit.
- Says and does things to indicate that she feels that someone is undeserving of an award or other recognition because that person does not work as hard or accomplish as much as she does.

- Expresses feelings that she should have what others have.

- Promotes herself at every opportunity.

- Points out where others are inferior or undeserving.

- Feels that she has to work harder for what she gets while others have it given to them.

- Feels that she is treated unfairly in comparison to others.

- Expresses that other people have it easier than she does.

Expects Favors

People with a DNP tend to have an expectation that others will do them favors, but these people should not expect any favors in return. It's almost like the destructive narcissist feels that they are making you a special person by getting you to do them a favor, and this should be reward enough for anyone. There is more than a hint of arrogance in this attitude.

Indices of Expecting Favors

Does your partner frequently do or say five or more of the following?

- Tells a child to get or do something for her, so that she doesn't have to move or stop what she is doing.

- Asks you to pick up something on your way home, when she could just as easily go and get it.

- Expects that others will do favors for her.

- Feels disappointed or rejected when someone refuses her a favor.

- Expects children to run personal errands for her.

- Expects you to use your leisure time doing things for her.

- Calls your family or friends for favors.

- Gets others to do things for her that she could do for herself.

- Becomes upset when someone fails to follow through on her request for a favor.

- Has unrealistic expectations when asking for favors.

Summary

This chapter focused on a general overview and description of the many behaviors and attitudes that, when clustered, are suggestive of a DNP. What you may find is that your partner has many of these troubling behaviors and attitudes, but not all of them. This is why chapters 5–8 present information to refine the descriptions by categorizing the DNP into four types. Also presented in these chapters are descriptions of how you may be adding to your distress with some behaviors and attitudes that are less than constructive and coping strategies for each type.

Although this chapter focused on behaviors and attitudes that described the characteristics for the Destructive Narcissistic Pattern for your partner, the same behaviors and attitudes could serve as a personal review of some undeveloped narcissism that you may have. That is, there are unconscious behaviors and attitudes you may have that are not as clustered, or as intense as those for a DNP, but could be affecting your relationships in negative ways. Use them as guidelines for making personal behavior changes.

Chapter 3

Your Characteristics,
Experiences, and Strengths

The previous chapters gave you information about indicators of being in a relationship with someone who has a Destructive Narcissistic Pattern, definitions and descriptions for behaviors and attitudes of destructive narcissism, and the major terms and concepts that will be explored in the remaining chapters.

We now turn to examining some personal characteristics you may have that are contributing to your reactions to the person with a DNP. These behaviors and attitudes are deep, long-standing, and may be unconscious. Some possible reasons for these will also be explored.

Personal Characteristics

As we begin to examine your personal characteristics, take note of the feelings aroused as you read and reflect on them. It could be enlightening to keep a journal of the thoughts, feelings, and ideas that are triggered for a more in-depth consideration at a later time. The intent, at this point, is only to establish some of the behaviors and attitudes that could be contributing to your distress and provide suggestions for possible changes.

Table 1: Personal Characteristics Scale

Directions: Rate yourself on each of the following items using the scale.

5—Always or almost always feel or do this
4—Frequently feel or do this
3—Sometimes feel or do this
2—Seldom feel or do this
1—Never or almost never do or feel this

1. Feel responsible for others' happiness	
2. Feel a personal failure when you don't perform as well as you think you should	
3. Feel worthless or guilty when criticized	
4. Fear the potential loss of the relationship with your partner	
5. Have high expectations for yourself and for others	
6. Are self-critical	
7. Fear being alone	
8. Have few sources of social support outside of family	
9. Have had disappointing relationships throughout your life	
10. Feel that you must take care of others' emotional needs	
Total _____	

Scoring

Add your ratings. Scores will range from 10–50. If your score is between 40–50, you have a considerable number of behaviors and attitudes that are contributing to your distress in your relationship and interactions with your partner; a score between 30–39 indicates many such behaviors and attitudes; a score between 20–29 indicates some of these behaviors and attitudes, but that they are not employed all of the time; and below 20 indicates few such behaviors and attitudes.

Responsible for Others' Happiness

If you rated yourself 3 or higher on this item, you may be assuming too much responsibility for others' happiness. The destructive narcissist can capitalize on your attitude and manipulate you to feel guilty for not making them pleased or happy. This feeling can be triggered without them having to say anything, because of your faulty assumption that you are responsible for someone else's happiness.

Personal Failure

Rating yourself 3+ on this item can indicate that you tend to think and feel that you have more control over your life, events, and experiences than is realistic. This faulty assumption leads you to feel guilt and shame for not being good enough when confronted with what you consider to be failure. You take responsibility even when it is apparent that you have little or no influence on the situation. Your partner can then easily arouse these feelings, because you are convinced that if you were better in some way you would have control and never fail. This is not realistic.

Feeling Worthless

This feeling can be distressing, as feeling worthless is more intense than just feeling you made a mistake. Feeling this way is a part of the impoverished self, in which you assume that others are more worthwhile than you are and/or that you lack something essential. You may do things that you don't want to do to prevent criticism, because being criticized triggers your feelings of worthlessness. Being discounted, demeaned, or devalued by your partner can increase the feeling of being worthless, and you will do almost anything to prevent feeling this way.

Potential Loss of the Relationship

Ratings of 3+ indicate considerable fear of losing the relationship, and you are alert and sensitive to this potential loss. You may even be convinced that your very survival is dependent on maintaining this relationship. Very high ratings on this item can signal deep issues around abandonment, and these should be worked through with a competent therapist. Suffice it to say that your issues around abandonment can contribute significantly to your distress.

High Expectations

Having high expectations for yourself and for others can be both positive and negative. High expectations can be positive, in the sense that you can work hard to achieve your ideals of perfection. High expectations can be negative, in the sense that you can be overly demanding and overly critical of anything less than perfection. This attitude, and the accompanying behavior, can make it difficult to satisfy you. Your destructive narcisstic partner can capitalize on this faulty assumption by pointing out mistakes, errors, and other deviations from perfection. You react by getting upset with yourself for not being perfect.

Self-Critical

The ability to perceive oneself realistically is an admirable trait, but engaging in self-examination may result in being overly critical. The discomfort that results from being critical can lead to positive changes. However, if you rated yourself 3+, you are likely engaging in self-criticism to an extent that is not helpful. You are being overly critical, and this self-perception can be used against you by your partner. Your partner will criticize you about the same things for which you are self-critical, add to those things, and produce some new ones. You are not able to counter these very effectively, because you have criticized yourself for some of them, and your partner is quick to point this out.

Fear of Being Alone

This fear can be so intense that you will do anything to prevent it from happening. You will negate and subjugate your needs, wishes, and values to keep from losing the relationship, because you intensely fear being alone. If you rated yourself 3+, you may be doing things that are not in your best interests, just to keep from being alone. This too, like item 4, can best be understood by working with a competent therapist. It is very similar to item 4, but differs in that you fear not only losing the relationship but also being alone. For the former, you may value the relationship so much that you fear its loss, while for the latter, you are convinced that you will be alone if your partner leaves. It's common or usual to feel lonely under these circumstances, but feeling alone implies isolation and alienation and that is not usual.

Few Sources of Social Support

It is helpful to have a robust support system. Good social support can prevent, reduce, and/or eliminate feelings of isolation and alienation. Our connections with others help us to keep from feeling lonely or cut off from meaning and purpose in our lives. Although, in an existential sense, we are alone, this does not mean that we have to feel lonely.

If you rated yourself as 3 or above, you may be feeling very isolated and adrift. You will want to examine your support system—family and friends whom you can count on for encouragement and support. Your support system is made up of the people whose care and respect you are sure of, and to whom you can go to in times of trouble, and they will welcome you. Each may play a different role, but all together they form a system of basic support for you. If you do not have such a support system, one coping and developmental strategy you can use is to begin to construct such a system.

Disappointing Relationships

There are very few adults who have not experienced at least one disappointing relationship in their lives. It is much more likely that there have been several of these in your life. The relationships referred to are not all romantic ones; they could be with parents, siblings, other family members, friends, and so on. This disappointment carries over into other relationships and affects your attitudes and behavior. For example, if you were betrayed in a previous relationship, you will fear and expect betrayal in subsequent relationships, which may lead you to be constantly alert to signs of potential betrayal. You may demand explanations, be suspicious, want a strict accounting of time and interactions, become more attentive, and engage in other acts designed to ward off what you consider to be potential betrayal. You are not able to trust your partner. Your partner then has an opportunity to manipulate you through your fear, say things that produce uncomfortable feelings in you, and keep you on edge. If you rated yourself 3+ on this item, you could benefit from some self-reflection on how previous betrayals impacted you and are influencing your current attitude and behaviors.

Taking Care of Others

Do you have a strong need or desire to take care of others, especially those who are perfectly capable of taking care of themselves? Do you rush to soothe when others become upset, or go out of your way not to do or say things that might get them upset? If you rated yourself 3+ on this item, you are overly caring for others and are putting yourself in a position to be exploited and manipulated. You may have an unconscious, faulty assumption that others are relying on you for their well-being, but this is seldom the case for adults. You may contribute to some extent to other adults' well-being, but they are not totally relying on you for their well-being. You are fostering dependence instead of independence. This is another issue that could be explored with a competent therapist.

These are but a few behaviors, attitudes, and faulty assumptions you may have that are contributing to your own distress in your relationship with your destructive narcissistic partner. The intent here is to increase your awareness of how your personal characteristics may be allowing the destructive narcissist's attitudes and behavior to affect you, explain why these attitudes and behaviors have a negative effect on you, and provide some suggestions for needed changes.

Experiences That Contribute to Your Reactions

It may not be enough for you to be aware of the personal characteristics, behaviors, and attitudes that contribute to your uncomfortable feelings and the openness to manipulation that is triggered and used so well by your destructive narcissistic partner. You need to know something about possible experiences from your past that could be contributors to the way you are today. This information can help you understand what happened and why it will be difficult to change your conscious behavior, as you are still responding to old parental messages and/or unfinished business. It's not impossible to change the influence of these things, but it's more difficult.

Table 2: My Experiences Scale

Directions: Begin by sitting in silence and reflecting on your growing years from the first thing you remember in childhood through adolescence. When you are ready, rate yourself on the following items using the scale.

5—Always or almost always experienced or felt this
4—Frequently experienced or felt this
3—Sometimes experienced or felt this
2—Seldom felt or experienced this
1—Never or almost never experienced or felt this

1. Made responsible for the emotional well-being of mother or father	
2. Mother or father were not emotionally present	
3. Felt lonely when growing up	
4. Experienced rejection by people close to you when you were growing up	
5. Experienced betrayal by people you thought cared for you	
6. Blamed for events and situations not under your control	
7. Felt devalued by mother or father	
8. Felt that something was lacking in your parent-child relationship when growing up	

9. Family life was chaotic	
10. Expected to know what your parents wanted or needed and give it to them without their having to verbalize it	
11. Parents compared you unfavorably with siblings or others	
12. Felt unhappy as a child and/or adolescent	
Total _____	

Scoring

Add your ratings to derive a total score. Scores will range from 12–60. If your rating fell between 49 and 60, you had a considerable number of negative experiences while growing up. A score between 40 and 48 indicates many such experiences; a score between 31 and 39 indicates some of these experiences; a score between 21 and 30 indicates few such experiences; and a score of 20 or below indicates that there were none or almost none of these negative experiences.

Parent's Well-Being

A child who is made responsible for a parent's well-being is what's known as a "parentified child" (Brown 2002). These children assume the parent's role of caring and nurturing, instead of the parent assuming that responsibility. All too often this occurs because the parent has underdeveloped narcissism, or even has a destructive narcissistic pattern. Their children are made to feel that they have to do or be what the parent wants if that parent is to be happy and pleased. Their children's whole existences are formed around what the parent wants, and the children are not free to search out and develop a unique identity (individuation). Their children are made to assume this role from birth, are unaware of any other way of being, and continue to act on this assumption with other people they meet throughout their lives.

Not Emotionally Present

There are many reasons why a parent is not or cannot be emotionally present for a child. Sometimes there is also a reason why the parent is not physically present, and this, too, prevents the parent from being emotionally present. Some reasons for physical and/or emotional absence include:

- military service,

- incarceration,

- death,

- parent's chronic illness,

- acute/chronic illness of an immediate family member,

- mental illness,

- depression, and

- employment that involves considerable travel or time commitments.

None of these involve deliberate attempts to be emotionally unavailable on the parent's part, but whether deliberate or not, the effects on the developing child can be significant.

The developing child can try harder to connect to the emotionally unavailable parent and, on an unconscious level, continue this pattern throughout life in their relationships with other people. Or, the child internalizes the notion that others are emotionally unavailable to connect with them, and thus will remain isolated and detached throughout life. Either way, if one or both parents were emotionally unavailable to you, this will have a significant impact on your current experience and relationships.

Lonely When Growing Up

This item is very similar to the previous one, but differs in some respects. Feeling lonely does not necessarily mean that the parent was emotionally unavailable, it simply means that you had feelings of loneliness. Some possible reasons for feeling lonely include:

- your parent may have been emotionally available sometimes, but you never knew when that would be,

- you may have had a childhood illness that kept you somewhat isolated,

- your parents divorced and one moved away, or

- you moved frequently.

It is not uncommon for children to feel lonely at some point. But it can have a negative impact when there are frequent or long periods of loneliness. The yearning for meaningful connections can then become so acute that you are willing to do things that are not in your best interest in order to hold on to a relationship that you think will give you the needed connection to ward off loneliness.

There is a vast difference between being alone and feeling lonely. Alone can be a time for revitalization, promotion of self-reflection, and introspection. It can be an opportunity to engage in creative pursuits, gain new information and new knowledge, practice meditation, and enjoy other positive activities. Lonely, on the other hand, implies a disconnection from others and the universe. This is an existential predicament that can produce much anxiety and fear. When you feel lonely, you experience being adrift in an unfriendly, inhospitable, and hostile universe and you fear that you will always remain in this state. Feeling lonely is also different from depression, as you may not experience many of the other negative effects associated with depression.

If you experienced the ache and yearning of loneliness when you were growing up, you may want to reflect on the extent to which this experience is influencing your current behaviors and attitudes. Further, you may also want to consider if this influence is causing you to be more amenable to manipulation by your destructive narcissistic partner.

Experienced Rejection

Rejection hurts. It is even more painful to a child because this rejection is perceived to happen because the child is not good enough, fatally flawed, and unworthy. Rejection promotes a whole host of associated feelings, such as:

- being devalued,

- anger and rage,

- wanting revenge,

- abandonment,

- terror,

- shame, and

- guilt.

While experiencing rejection by a parent can be the ultimate rejection, other people who are rejecting also produce pain.

The pain and other uncomfortable feelings associated with rejection never fade, but can become transformed, repressed, and displaced. For example, you may try to not put yourself in a place where you will be rejected. You may become what the other person wants or needs, or you may act against your values and principles. You may not be consciously aware that you do these things to avoid being rejected, as this most likely remains on an unconscious level.

You may want to examine your behavior in your relationships as an adolescent and as an adult to see if any of these unconscious responses to rejection were influential. You may also benefit from assessing if these responses produced the desired result, if you are continuing to use them in your current relationship with your partner, and if they are any more effective today than they were in the past.

Experienced Betrayal

If you experienced betrayal, you may have an inability to trust, a fear of intimacy, an expectation that you will be betrayed again, and many negative feelings about your self-worth. When someone betrays your trust, you lose innocence, faith in others' goodness, and self-confidence. There are numerous negative effects, and these also impact your relationships. Some possible effects include:

- becoming overly suspicious,

- trying to hold on to the other person's affections too tightly,

- seeking to prove you are worthy, and that the person who betrayed you was wrong,

- entering into relationships too quickly,

- becoming superficial in your relationships,

- staying on edge and expecting the worst at all times,

- becoming challenging about the least little thing, and

- refusing to let others get too close.

Any of these can provide your destructive narcissistic partner with many opportunities to point out your errors and flaws, leading to your feeling even more distress.

What is likely to be happening is that you are perceiving the "new" in terms of the "old." The new constitutes those relationships after the betrayal, and you act in these relationships as if they were the old relationship where the betrayal occurred. Understanding what you are doing, such as being unable to trust, is the first step toward learning how to let go of the past, forgive but not necessarily forget, and see the new more objectively.

Blame

If you were frequently or almost always blamed for things that were out of your control, you've probably developed one of two responses you use today when challenged or blamed—acceptance or defiance. You either accept blame when it's not really justified or you refuse to ever accept any blame even if it is justified. Neither response is constructive, nor helpful for your relationships.

What probably happened is that you had one or both parents who planted the messages that you were to blame if things went wrong, that you were not good enough to prevent these things from happening, and that you were fatally flawed. These messages, when internalized, can produce easily triggered guilt and shame. The accepting response triggers overwhelming guilt and shame, and others can use these responses to manipulate you. The defiant response wards off these feelings, but opens you up to charges of failure to assume responsibility for your mistakes and makes you appear to be arrogant. The attitude that is conveyed is that you never make mistakes, and this cannot be true.

Your destructive narcissistic partner can have an easy time triggering your guilt and shame or pointing out your arrogance. Either way, you end up with very uncomfortable feelings.

Feeling Devalued

It is important for our self-esteem that we feel appreciated and valued as worthwhile, unique persons. Part of how our self-concept develops includes how others treat us, beginning at birth. The mother-child relationship (or parent-caretaker) is a vital and critical one for the child. How the child is taken care of, responded to, accepted, and valued, or not, by the mother sends powerful messages that are incorporated into the self. This is the beginning of forming one's self-concept, and carries the basic messages about how you perceive yourself. Others throughout your life have varying levels of impact and influence on your self-concept, but it is this early relationship that lays the foundation.

After becoming an adult, you should be able to effectively handle others' attempts to devalue you, and not have these acts affect your feelings about yourself. You don't have to feel devalued, unless you buy into the notion that you are less worthy, that you may be flawed, that others do not want you, and that you are of little or no consequence. These negative self-statements are not helpful for your self-confidence, self-esteem, and self-perception.

What can happen, as a part of feeling devalued, is that you redouble your efforts to please the person who says or does things that produce the devaluing feelings. You may even do things you do not want to do in an effort to please, and your hope is that the person will value and want you. This yearning for acceptance and being valued may not be in your best interests, and may be part of why you are reacting as you do to your destructive narcissistic partner.

Deficits in Early Relationships

If you rated yourself 3+ on this item, you may have experienced one or more of the following: being a parentified child, emotionally distant parents, parental rejection, neglect, or lack of empathy for your concerns. It is not unusual for a parent to be distracted, or to have crises or major concerns and other temporary conditions that make them less attentive and accessible. You felt the loss, but they did return and give you attention, care, and emotional support. If you still feel there was something lacking, this loss was chronic and long-term.

A long-term condition that resulted in your feeling there was a deficit in the relationship has implications for your relationships throughout your life. These implications take many forms, such as:

- trying to correct the early deficit in other relationships,

- needing to be closer and more intimate than others can tolerate,

- a fear of connecting to others,

- a constant concern that others too will be emotionally unavailable,

- yearning for the unavailable connection and seeking it in self-destructive ways, and

- doing things you do not want to do, so that the other person will remain available and connected.

Reflect on your behaviors and attitudes with your partner. See if any or all of these are influences on you and have implications for the relationship. These are deep-seated and long lasting, which can make it difficult for you to make changes. You may need the guidance of a competent mental health professional to work through your feeling this deficit, in order to change your current behaviors and attitudes.

Chaotic Family Life

Inconsistent behavior, not knowing what to expect, swings between extremes of mood, and not understanding what was expected of you are some indices of chaotic family life. Whatever manifestation the chaos took, it had an impact on you that persists to this day.

Growing up in a chaotic family could result in your not having developed a secure basis for expectations of self and of others. You could never predict what would happen, or could not rely on others' responses to be consistent or predictable, and these situations produced a considerable amount of inner insecurity. This inner state affected your sense of self and the quality and kinds of relationships you formed, and continues to influence you and your life in many ways. Some possible outcomes are:

- an inability to trust,

- a reluctance to let your real self be known,

- holding back of emotions and of their expression while searching for security,

- a rigidity of expectations for others,

- a strong need for safety in relationships,

- a tendency to be edgy and ever alert, and

- trying to read others' minds and respond quickly to what you think they want.

These are the kinds of behaviors and attitudes that can aid a destructive narcissist partner in controlling, manipulating, and exploiting you. These are deep-seated issues and concerns that are best worked through with a competent therapist.

Mind Reading

Did one or more of your parents frequently say any of the following to you?

- "You should have known what I wanted."

- "I shouldn't have to tell you what I need from you."

- "You should know what to do without my telling you."

- "Why didn't you do _____? You know that I expected that of you."

- "You should know all this. You don't need me to tell you."

Did your parents expect you to understand their needs, wants, and desires and to fulfill these without instructions, directions, orders, or requests? Were you made to feel inadequate for failing to do these? Were you blamed for being flawed because you did not meet their expectations for mind reading?

If the above resonates with you, then you grew up in a family where you were expected to read others' minds and do what they expected, and you were blamed and criticized when you failed, read them wrong, or ignored them. These experiences had an impact on you that persists to this day.

Emotional attunement can be very satisfying, as the other person does seem to anticipate what you want or need, and tries to give it to you. You feel that person really cares for you, and you value the connection. This can be especially important in the parent/child relationship for the child, as it builds a sense of security, safety, and love. On the rare occasions when this happens with others as you grow up, you are pleased and gratified. This is not what is meant by mind reading, because you do not have an expectation that the other person should, or must, be emotionally attuned to you. You appreciate it, but you do not demand it. If you are expecting or demanding it, it will have a negative effect on your relationships.

One source of possible discomfort between you and your destructive narcissistic partner could be his expectation that you will read his mind and react accordingly. When you do not, or cannot, this lapse becomes a point of contention. If you grew up in a home where mind reading was an expectation, your reactions will most likely be guilt and shame. If your family did not expect mind reading, your reactions are most likely confusion and anger. None of these are constructive responses, and they arise because of an incomplete understanding on both your parts of the expectation for mind reading.

Unfavorable Comparisons

Parents sometimes unwittingly or deliberately promote jealousy, shame, or competitive feelings by making unfavorable comparisons between you, and other people, such as your siblings. If you rated this item 3+, then you felt you were often compared unfavorably with others. The accompanying negative feelings can be easily triggered today, when you feel your partner is comparing you with others, especially when that comparison has an unfavorable reflection on you.

Comparisons with others, either when you or someone else is doing it, can be counterproductive and point to an unrealistic expectation for self. You, or the other person, are either focused on how you don't measure up or on how others cannot measure up to you. Neither is helpful to you or to your relationships.

If this is a behavior of your partner, then they are most likely trying to get you to change to meet their needs, using this as a means of controlling you, seeking to demoralize you, or pointing out how unsatisfactory you are. There does not appear to be any positive reason for making these unfavorable comparisons.

But you must be careful when considering this behavior, as you may be inferring that unfavorable comparisons are being made when your partner is simply complimenting or admiring something about another person. Compliments and admiring comments do not always carry an overt or indirect comparison, and you may be reacting to your old parental messages, instead of being realistic and objective about the comments. It could be helpful to adopt the position that only direct statements by your partner that compare you unfavorably with others receive a response. Indirect comments are ignored. Suggestions for constructive reactions and responses are presented in chapter 9.

Unhappy Childhood

This is a rather global item, where you are asked to rate the level and extent of your happiness as you were growing up. The overall rating lets you begin to become aware of what you are searching for in your current relationships, what you feel you missed during your formative years, and how you may have unrealistic expectations and unreasonable demands for your relationships. It can also provide cues for why you were captivated, and continue to be captivated, by your partner.

Most everyone had some unhappy times or moments during childhood and adolescence. Some people, when reflecting on those years, become more aware of the impact of distressing events, whereas before they had minimized them. Others become aware that, in spite of some unhappy events, they would characterize these periods as happy, or at least not unhappy. Each person differs in their perspective.

However, these periods of your life are your foundation years and set a pattern for your self-perception, self-confidence, and for what you want and need from your relationships.

Your destructive narcissistic partner can capitalize on your yearnings, needs, and desires and give you enough reason to hope that he can fulfill them. He can also use these to trigger your unconscious guilt and shame for not being good enough to have happiness.

You cannot change the past, nor can you change what happened to you, no matter how traumatic it was. Your life events are an integral part of you, and helped form the kind of person you are today. What can be changed are the negative impacts of these events on you and your relationships. You can make conscious choices about your behavior and attitudes and work to become the kind of person you want to be. This is not easy to do, and the life events you experienced may need to be explored in therapy for a more complete understanding and resolution. The first step is awareness of what about you needs work, an acceptance that work is needed, and a willingness to engage in self-exploration. The material in this book can guide you to increased awareness.

Summary

You now have a better idea of the personal characteristics and experiences that may be contributing to your distress. Yes, your partner who has a DNP is doing and saying things that are troubling, upsetting, or even infuriating, but you are experiencing some of your feelings because of old parental messages, early experiences, unresolved family of origin issues, and other unfinished business. Let's begin to focus on helping you to understand, fortify, and build yourself, and to develop coping and protective strategies. Neither you, nor I, can change your partner. What can be done is for you to become more understanding of yourself, your partner, and the relationship, and to be better able to cope with some of their troubling behaviors and attitudes.

Self-Strengths

Your major source for change will be your inner resources and strengths. You can build on these to develop coping and protective strategies, and to aid in personal growth and development. While you may be aware and use many of your strengths, you are likely to have others that remain unrecognized and underused. Thus, we need to find out what your unknown strengths may be. The following scale can help you identify some strengths.

Table 3: Identifying Self-Strengths

Directions: Rate yourself on the following items using the scale.

5—Always or very much like you
4—Frequently or much like you
3—Sometimes or occasionally like you
2—Seldom or not much like you
1—Never, almost never, or nothing like you

1. I am able to say what is bothering me rather than burying these feelings	
2. I am able to appropriately express a wide range of feelings, both positive and negative	
3. I can express mild feelings (for example, irritation)	
4. I can recognize when I am uncertain of what I am feeling and can express that	
5. When I express my feelings, I stay in touch with the impact on the receiver	
6. I can express my feelings without blaming someone for causing the feelings	
7. I try to express my feelings without being judgmental	
8. I am able and willing to be assertive	
9. I do not do things that I feel violate my beliefs or principles	
10. I do not do things that others want me to do, but I don't want to do	
11. I will stand up for what I believe	
12. I am self-reflective, but not self-blaming, when I make a mistake	
13. I am able to delay self-gratification	
14. I can forgive my mistakes	

15. I accept personal responsibility for my mistakes, choices, and decisions	
16. I am able to step back and objectively look at my behavior or attitude	
17. I am generous with my time and resources	
18. I seek out and maintain intimate relationships	
19. I work hard to achieve my goals	
20. After I fail at something, I will try again	
Total _____	

Scoring

Add your ratings. Scores will range from 20–100. A total score between 85–100 indicates that you feel you have considerable personal strengths from which you can pull to make effective changes. A score between 70–84 indicates that you feel you have many such strengths. A score between 55–69 indicates that you feel you have a modest number of these strengths. A score between 40–54 indicates that you feel you have few such strengths. A score below 40 suggests that you feel you have none or almost none of these.

Feelings and Expressions

Items 1–7 focus on your awareness of your personal feelings and your ability to openly express them. Along with awareness and expression comes appropriateness. That is, you have some sense of what feelings are appropriate to express, your means of expression are suitable for the other person and the place, and you take timing into account when expressing your feelings.

If you rated yourself 4 or 5 on most of these items, you can use these strengths to develop protective and coping strategies. If you rated yourself below 4 on any item, you can use that particular behavior or attitude and work to strengthen it. For example, if you rated yourself 3 on item 3 (Can express mild feelings), then I encourage you to work to increase your awareness of when you are experiencing a mild version of a feeling and begin to openly express it at that time. One outcome for increasing your ability in this area is that you can often prevent the mild version from escalating and intensifying. An illustration of this is seen when becoming aware of and expressing irritation, which can prevent it from becoming anger or fury. You can control a mild feeling better than you can the more intense version. Further, you are less likely to become paralyzed, overwhelmed, or enmeshed by the mild version, whereas you could experience any or all of these with the more intense version. This is just one example of why and how making these items part of your strength resources could be helpful.

Speaking Out

Items 8–11 focus on your speaking up or out for what you want or need, and on your willingness to allow yourself to be manipulated to meet others' needs. Being assertive, and not aggressive or passive, is a major strength when interacting with anyone who has a DNP. Not compromising your beliefs, values, or principles is another personal strength that can help you feel better about yourself and enable you to deal with guilt and shame triggered by your destructive narcissistic partner.

If you rated yourself 4–5 on each of these items, you have behaviors and attitudes in place that can be helpful to you. Ratings below 4 on any item indicate that you could work to enhance the behavior or attitude. Pay special attention to any item rated 1 or 2. These need particular attention, as you are not using some behaviors and attitudes that could help you better cope with your partner. These also play a major role in your positive self-esteem.

Self-Talk

Items 12–16 focus on some ways in which you think about yourself and point out some aspects of maturity. If you rated yourself 4 or 5 on each of the items, then you are very positive in your self-talk and certain aspects of mature behaviors and attitudes. Items rated 3 or less could use some attention and strengthening.

Two of the most negative outcomes for being in a relationship with a destructive narcissist are the erosion of your self-confidence and of your self-esteem. You can begin to doubt your competence, efficacy, and even your sanity. You start to second-guess and question what is real and who you are. If you are able to rate yourself 4 or 5 on these items, you will be less affected by these negative comments, as you don't add to them with negative self-talk. If you rate yourself 3 and below, you will want to work to strengthen these behaviors and attitudes to make them major assets for you.

Reaching Out to Others

Items 17 and 18 speak of your ability to reach out to others and make significant connections. Item 17 can be an indication of altruism, where you give of yourself to others, and item 18 is about the quality of your other relationships. Rating yourself 4 or 5 indicates you feel some satisfaction and success in these areas. They can also be assets on which you can build. Ratings of 3 or below can indicate that you are not reaching out to others as much as you could. This is an area where you could be more effective.

Determination and Persistence

The last two items relate to determination and persistence, two characteristics that will enable you to effectively use protective and coping strategies with your destructive narcissistic partner. You will need to persist even if it appears that your strategies are not as effective as you would like them to be, as it takes time for you to become comfortable with them. If you rated yourself 4 or 5, you are satisfied with your determination and persistence. If you rated yourself 3 or below, you will need to remind yourself to be patient and to use some self-affirming statements to bolster your persistence. These will also be very helpful to enable you to make needed changes in your behavior and attitudes.

Summary

As you worked through the scale, you should have become much more aware of your strengths. You may even have identified some that are not on the list. What you do not want to have as your primary focus is emphasizing remediation of perceived deficiencies. Yes, there may be some and you will want to do some work on those, but the most effective and constructive approach is to use your strengths. Many of the exercises in the book are focused on increasing your awareness of your strengths and enhancing them.

Chapter 4

Communication Strategies and Basic Grounding

Specific coping and protective strategies for each of the four types of DNP are presented in chapters 5–8. Presented here are some basic strategies that can be used with every type. These are useful if your partner seems not to fit any of the types, or when you can see characteristics for every type of in them. Coping in this discussion refers to what you can think or do that will help you reduce or eliminate the negative impact of some of your partner's behaviors and attitudes. Protective strategies are those that can help you deal with the immediate reactions you have when you interact with your partner. Read these strategies with the understanding that you can choose those that fit your personality and situation. Some suggestions will not seem to fit at first, and you are not expected to adopt them all. It is suggested that you come back to those that do not seem to fit at some point and reconsider how or if you can make any use of them.

Communication Strategies

Let's begin with some strategies that can be of assistance in the short term to allow you to have more constructive interactions with your partner, prevent you from having unpleasant feelings triggered or intensified, and permit you to be more satisfied with yourself. Additional strategies arise as a result of building and developing yourself, reducing your underdeveloped narcissism, and fostering the growth of your healthy adult narcissism. The self-development strategies are presented in chapter 9. This discussion focuses on communication, understanding your psychological boundaries, and other relationship strategies.

It is difficult to discuss communication strategies as protection, because a cornerstone for satisfying intimate relationships would focus on the quality of communications. The same communication skills that are usually presented for fostering and strengthening relationships are counterproductive if you are in a relationship with a destructive narcissist. Let's take a look at these communication skills. First, think of a satisfying relationship you have, or had, with an adult and focus on the pattern of communication between you and that person. That communication pattern was probably characterized by both of you doing many or all of the following:

- Maintaining mutual interest and respect.

- Attending to or focusing on the speaker.

- Screening out distractions.

- Letting the other person finish their thoughts or statements and not interrupting.

- Demonstrating empathy.

- Feeling that you were heard and understood.

- Experiencing the absence of, or very infrequent, criticism or blame.

- Attempting to understand each other's perspective.

- Not making deliberately misleading statements or lies.

- Exhibiting a willingness to let the real self be known.

Unfortunately, communication with your partner can lack many of these and is probably frustrating and unsatisfying.

Mutual Interest and Respect

The keywords here are mutual and respect. You probably give your partner interest and respect, and expect to receive the same in return. You may even yearn to return to what you perceived as interest and respect in the beginning stage of your relationship. The trouble is that your perception was most likely off target. What you perceived as interest and respect was most likely her response to your behaviors and attitudes that did most of the following:

- Mirrored her grandiosity or inflated self-perception.
- Gave her your undivided attention.
- Admired her as she desired to be admired.
- Let her know that you considered her to be unique and special.
- Accepted intrusive intimacy.
- Empathized with her.
- Excused or rationalized any inconsiderate acts or lies.

Once you decreased or stopped any of these, your partner's interest in you was gone. You were unaware of the absence at first, because you thought you were both adjusting to each other and that the relationship had a basic mutuality. It did not. Some of your dissatisfaction with your partner is because her interactions show a lack of interest and respect. But what you did not realize was that you never had real mutuality, and are unlikely to develop it. This is one of the yearnings and fantasies you have to relinquish.

Attending

When you focus on a speaker by giving them eye contact, orienting your body toward them, and giving them your attention, you promote connection, convey interest, and allow the person to feel valued. These are all positive behaviors and attitudes for satisfying communications. However, these same actions work against you in interactions with your destructive narcissist partner, because they allow your partner to intrude upon, violate, and destroy your psychological boundaries. Boundary strength is what protects you from external assaults, such as projections, and from internal assaults, such as having guilt and shame triggered.

One quick and simple step you can institute is to reduce the times when you are *attending* to your partner. These include:

- don't allow eye contact,
- orient your body away from her,
- put slightly more physical space between the two of you, and

- pay only partial attention.

Save the full attending for those times when communications are more satisfying and pleasant. Make a practice of not attending fully until you are sure which way the interaction is heading. If you are wrong in your analysis, you can employ your emotional shield, which will be described later in the chapter.

Distractions

Another strategy that can keep you from fully attending and reduce your susceptibility to projections and manipulations is to become distracted. Distractions can be:

- a change of topic,

- thinking about other things,

- turning to look at something in the vicinity, and so forth.

You are not fully emotionally present for the interaction, and that can protect you.

Good communication skills would have you screen out distractions, be emotionally present, and attend to the speaker. What you may be experiencing when you use these good communicating skills with your partner is that you often end up frustrated, feeling manipulated, having your guilt and shame triggered, and being left with a number of unpleasant feelings after the interaction is finished. You may even have increased your efforts at better communication, but found that it did not work. It may be helpful for you to try being distracted for some interactions. This can give you an opportunity to see if being distracted would improve how you felt after interactions and result in less unpleasant and troubling feelings.

Interrupting

When you finish others' statements, you are interrupting. Sometimes, this is "putting words in their mouth" instead of letting them express their thoughts and feelings in their way. Interrupting can lead the person to feel that you are conveying some, or all, of the following:

- not valuing your partner,

- not respecting your partner,

- feeling superior and more knowledgeable,

- considering your partner incompetent or stupid,

- being impatient,

- not willing to try to understand what your partner is conveying or means, and

- not wanting to hear what your partner has to say.

In short, when you interrupt the speaker, you are not using good communication skills. Interrupting is an effective strategy to use with your destructive narcissist partner on those occasions when you find yourself getting very upset at what your partner is saying. If you do interrupt, do so by changing the subject or saying something off the wall. Do not interrupt to defend yourself or to attack your partner. Defending and attacking are how disagreements escalate into more intense conflicts. Furthermore, defending yourself or attacking your partner will not result in constructive outcomes.

Empathy

When you empathize, you open yourself to another person and feel or sense their feelings, but do not lose yourself in their feelings. You are still aware that you are separate and distinct from the other person. If you become enmeshed or overwhelmed by other people's emotions, you lack sufficient boundary strength, and this lack allows you to get lost in other people's feelings. If this happens to you, then this is not empathy; this is enmeshment or being overwhelmed.

It can be enriching to a relationship when each person shows empathy to the other. If only one partner is empathetic, it can detract from the quality of the relationship. This is one reason why empathy is listed with good communication skills. Many relationships thrive precisely because there is sufficient empathy on both people's parts.

However, if you are in a relationship with a destructive narcissist, you probably get little or no empathy. And, if your boundaries are not strong enough, you can experience being enmeshed and overwhelmed by your partner's projections and projective identifications when you open yourself to try and empathize.

A strategy that can help is to *restrict your attempts to empathize with your partner.* Use a more cognitive or thinking kind of understanding instead of allowing yourself to feel what your partner is feeling. If you feel your boundaries need strengthening, you can use emotional shielding, but do not try to empathize with your partner until you can do so without losing yourself in their feelings.

Heard and Understood

This characteristic and skill is closely related to empathy, but is a little more remote and cognitive. Feeling heard and understood enhances a relationship and is especially helpful if both members in the relationship feel this way. What leads you to believe that someone heard and understood you? Whatever the situation or topic, the other person probably did all or most of the following.

- Looked at you when you were talking.

- Remained focused on you.

- Responded directly and verbally to what you were saying.

- Used words to acknowledge what you said by paraphrasing or repeating.

- Did not argue, disagree, or challenge you before acknowledging your response. That is, the person first acknowledged what you were saying.

- In instances where there were differences of opinion or thought, the other person took care to try to hear what you were saying.

Do any of these seem familiar to your interaction with your partner? Or, are these interactions one-sided, with you doing most or all of the above? Do you feel heard and understood much of the time? What can you do that will help you continue to hear and understand, but not feel so discounted and devalued by your partner's response and failure to reciprocate? Here are two suggestions:

- Stop the responding process at paraphrasing or repeating.

- Give up your fantasy of reciprocity.

You probably don't want to just ignore your partner and not respond at all, although this is an option. If you do choose to ignore what your partner is saying, use this strategy judiciously, as it is unlikely to help the relationship. What you can do is to repeat or paraphrase what your partner says to let your partner know that you are attentive and that you hear what they are saying. You don't have to do anything more than that. Do not volunteer your perspective, use soothing words, give suggestions to "fix" whatever it is, or provide explanations. Keep the focus on what your partner is saying.

The second suggestion may be harder to implement; that is, to give up your yearning and expectation for reciprocity. If it should ever happen you can be relieved. But this is unlikely, and your continued expectation is hurting you, not your partner.

Criticism and Blame

Feelings of guilt and shame are aroused by criticism and blame, and these feelings do not contribute to positive communications and relationships. The targets of criticism or blame usually feel flawed, wrong, inept, incompetent, unacceptable, and a host of other negative feelings. When the intent of an interaction is to foster a closer relationship, each person makes an attempt to reduce, limit, or eliminate criticism or blame.

However, your destructive narcissist partner probably does not exercise restraint in making criticizing and blaming comments to and about you. You may also find yourself in the position of frequently explaining or defending yourself, fighting back with criticism and blame for your partner, getting mad, and withdrawing or sulking. Some destructive narcissist partners may even have an attitude that implies that you are so lucky to have someone like them, given that you are so flawed and inferior. You can't feel very good about yourself or the relationship in that instance.

What can you do when facing criticism or blame? First, you can understand that these comments are simply triggering old parental messages that, in turn, arouse your guilt and shame. Working to reduce or eliminate these effects is best done with a competent therapist, as that exploration and self-examination is long-term. For the immediate future, you can do one or more of the following:

- Employ your emotional insulation (discussed later in this chapter).

- Appear to agree with the comments.

- Deflect the course of the conversation.

- Refuse to react with hurt or shame.

- Say you'll do better next time.

- Focus your thoughts on your strengths.

- Withdraw.

- Think about something else.

Don't get mired in the distressing feelings that were aroused, and don't openly express your feelings of guilt and shame. That will only reinforce your partner's negative perception and comments.

Each Other's Perspective

When there is constructive and effective two-way communication, each person involved attempts to understand the other's perspective. You probably have practiced this understanding with your partner, but did not receive any attempt on your partner's part to understand your perception. Face it, the constructive communication behavior in your relationship is a one-way deal. You are not receiving the same consideration you give. The likelihood that your pointing out this discrepancy to your partner will bring about desired changes is slim or none. Persons with a DNP generally cannot see any perspective but their own and do not understand how this stance affects their relationships.

It can be difficult for you to accept that nothing can be done to get your partner to even try to understand your perspective. That's right, nothing you say or do can get through to your partner, and you waste your time and effort when you continue this futile pursuit. You also increase your frustration, and other negative feelings, because your attempts fail. You may intensify your attempts or try new ones, but they too fail. You may be the kind of person who takes this failure personally and you may berate yourself for not being more effective. This too is futile and counterproductive. You were doomed to failure from the very beginning, and this failure is not due to any personal deficit of yours. No one could get through. Your destructive narcissistic partner has very strong defenses to keep everyone away, and neither you, nor anyone else, can get through. Fight other battles, as you cannot win this one.

Misleading Statements and Lies

Relationships are strengthened when there is open, clear, direct, and truthful communication on the part of both parties. Relationships are weakened and become unsatisfactory when these are absent. You probably make every effort to be truthful and not make misleading statements to your partner, only to find that your partner is not so careful with you.

Destructive narcissists categorized as "Manipulative" are particularly prone to use misleading statements and lies. Do they know they are lying? Yes. But, they feel they have the right to use any means available to achieve their ends. Further, some will have an assumption, much like that of "Suspicious" narcissists, that everyone is lying, and thus lying is fair play.

One of the most infuriating and frustrating things that can happen is that your challenges are often turned back on you, and you end up being wrong. For example, your partner says that your boss called, left you a message about a meeting, and seemed annoyed. You ask your partner what did the boss say that conveyed his annoyance, and your partner gives you a blow by blow of what was said and how it was said. You accept your partner's judgment. At the meeting the next day, you are prepared for the boss's annoyance, but look in vain for the signs. To help diffuse what you think will be annoyance, you decide to delay bringing up an issue that is very important for you. The boss is very cordial toward you during the meeting and shows no signs of being annoyed. That evening, you tell your partner how well the meeting went, and your partner asks you why you thought it wouldn't go well. Your response is that your partner had said that the boss was annoyed when he had called, and you were prepared to deal with that. Your partner then denies having said any such thing and cannot imagine where you got that notion. You try to refute what your partner says, but you are upset and your partner is calm. You lose the argument and are left with a number of unpleasant feelings.

Unfortunately, the only strategies that will help you are those that require you to become suspicious and disbelieving. You cannot trust that your partner is truthful or accurate, and you have to be skeptical and verify their accuracy. It's best not to be open about your need to check out the validity of what your partner tells you, as this would lead to a charge of mistrust, hurt feelings, and blaming you for being suspicious.

The Real Self

The strength of a relationship can be gauged by the extent to which both partners are willing to let their real self be known. This is the innermost part of you and can be easily hurt. This part of you is revealed only to people you trust and with whom you feel safe. Your intimate partner is one person you hope or think fits this description, and you allow some or all of your real self to be seen by your partner. The expectation is that your partner will reciprocate and allow you to see their real self. You realize over time that you have opened yourself, but that your partner has not. Your partner repels all attempts to get closer and you cannot understand why you are being shut out.

You may have to accept that you will never have the kind of intimate relationship where your partner will allow her real self to be known. Your partner cannot let those barriers down to the extent that you can, and even with considerable personal work on her part, may not achieve that state or goal. Your task is difficult, as you must be willing to do all or most of the following:

- Accept your partner as she is.

- Refrain from pushing or demanding that your partner let you in.

- Realize that your relationship cannot have the level of intimacy that you desire.

- Work on controlling your need to have your partner's real self revealed to you.

Grounding Strategies

The strategies discussed in this section call for you to do a lot of self-reflection and self-examination, so that you can select the ones that best fit your needs, personality, and situation. Several possible strategies are presented, and all may not be suitable for you. As you read about each, consider the following questions:

- How comfortable will it be for you to try to use this strategy?

- Will it make you feel worse or make the situation worse?

- What would be some possible benefits of using this strategy?

- What are some possible positive and negative effects on the relationship?

Comfort with a strategy is not a prerequisite, as experimenting with new behavior is almost always uncomfortable and anxiety producing. You can expect some degree of discomfort, but that should not deter you from trying a particular strategy. What can be important, however, is to select those strategies that may cause you some mild discomfort at first, but which are consistent with your personality, so that this discomfort will be reduced or eliminated at some point. Other reasons for using strategies consistent with your personality are that you are likely to be able to see how they can be easily instituted and how you can persist in using them.

You don't want to do anything that may cause you to feel worse than you ordinarily feel or that makes the situation worse. There may be some initial discomfort, but it should be mild and manageable. Carefully reflect on what you think you would feel, how your partner would likely react, and what effect the strategy would have on the relationship.

You will want to select strategies that you feel would have positive benefits. That may seem obvious, but it takes some thought and understanding to examine each strategy and to note the pros and cons before deciding to use or reject it. You will want to pay particular attention to any personal positive benefits, such as reduction of your feelings of guilt or shame. The reduction of stress on you, your family life, and on the relationship could be very beneficial.

Another consideration when reviewing strategies is the possible effect on the relationship. You are in the best position to decide if an effect would be positive or negative, and this can be a major consideration for your decision to use, or not use, a particular strategy.

The first group of strategies is intended to have a grounding and stabilizing effect on you and the relationship. They have some additional benefits, such as the following:

- Keeping conflict from escalating.

- Protecting you from your partner's projections.

- Protecting you from identifying with and acting on your partner's projections.

- Reducing or eliminating many triggered unpleasant feelings.

- Promoting a sense of self-efficacy.

- Allowing you some space and time for reflection and self-examination.

The following strategies are recommended for everyone and you can make modifications to them to suit you and your particular situation. These grounding strategies are:

- emotional insulation,

- deciding not to confront your partner,

- acceptance of your partner as she is,

- changing your attitude and expectations, and

- securing an ally.

Emotional Insulation

This strategy allows you to screen out the projections of others, reduce projective identifications, and to constrain your triggered feelings, such as guilt and shame. Think about a recent unsatisfactory interaction with your destructive narcissist partner. The discussion probably started off satisfactorily; you were not angry or carrying another intense feeling. However, as you continued the discussion, you found yourself becoming very upset and remained so long after the discussion ended. You may have experienced a taking in, identifying with, and acting on a projection from your partner, and that is called projective identification. Emotional insulation would prevent that from happening.

Use the following exercise to develop your emotional insulation. Read all the instructions before beginning the exercise.

Grounding Exercise 1: *My Insulation*

Materials: A sheet of paper, a pencil, and crayons or felt markers in a variety of colors.

Directions: Sit in silence in a place where you will not be disturbed. Don't try to think of anything; simply try to clear your mind. Clearing your mind can be helped if you concentrate on your breathing and try to breathe deeply and evenly.

As you sit in silence, allow the image of a barrier between you and your partner to emerge. This barrier screens out the negative comments and projections, while allowing the positive to get through. Explore this barrier and see its shape, colors, height, width, depth, and weight. Establish as many descriptive characteristics for your barrier as you can. When you are ready, open your eyes and draw that image, including its color. Drawing can help "fix" the image and make it more real for you.

The barrier you imagined and drew is the one you can use as emotional insulation. The most effective use is to visualize it before interacting with your partner. It can still be effective if employed during an interaction, but it is not as effective if you wait. If you forget to visualize it prior to interaction, you can always do it during the interchange. Use it to prevent your partner's projections, because once the projections cannot get through, many of your unpleasant feelings will not be triggered, or they will be less intense. The other piece of work you can do is to better understand, manage, and contain these unpleasant feelings. That work is beyond the scope and intent of this book, and can best be done with a competent therapist.

Do Not Confront

Regardless of how you define confronting, it is in your best interest to make a practice of not confronting your destructive narcissistic partner. You've probably tried it in the past, and it did not work to your benefit or satisfaction. The truth is, it will never work.

Confrontation, at its best, should not be:

- an attack,
- telling someone off,
- off-loading resentment or blame,
- illustrating your superiority and another person's inferiority,
- a way to show off, or
- making people aware of their flaws.

These are all forms of destructive confrontation, and some of them may fit what you have as a motive for confronting your partner.

You probably psyched yourself up to confront your partner, and did so in the hope that your partner would finally be able to see their troubling behavior and attitudes. What most likely happened is that your partner was unresponsive to your concern, turned your confrontation back on you, and you ended up feeling worse than you did when you started. This pattern will repeat itself, since the destructive narcissist is blind to the impact that her behavior and attitudes have on others. The destructive narcissist considers others as the problem and will attack or become defensive at the least hint of criticism. She can be contemptuous of anyone she does not feel is superior to her. A confrontation does not work and you are much better off if you just give up trying to confront.

Acceptance

Your situation will become more tolerable if you can bring yourself to accept your partner as is. This may seem trite and redundant, but part of your distress comes from unsuccessful attempts to change your partner. You may deny to yourself and to others that you want to change your partner, but, in reality, you do want your partner to change. You particularly want the changes that impact you.

It will be difficult to understand that people like your partner are doing the very best that they can, and that it will take a personal commitment on their part to effect any changes. You cannot do it for them, and no amount of pleading, talking, or threats will cause them to change. Think of acceptance in this way. You are going to give your partner what she did not get from her early life: acceptance for who she is. That doesn't mean that you must agree with everything your partner says, nor accept verbal or emotional abuse. No, it only means that you cease fighting, encouraging, or whatever you are doing to try to change your partner. (Note: By no means should you ever accept physical abuse.)

Your Attitude and Expectations

You will make progress toward acceptance of your partner and implement effective strategies if you are able to change your attitude and expectations. Needed changes are somewhat individualistic, call for self-reflection and self-examination, and can only be presented here in global terms. You will have to decide for yourself, if or how to change. Some possible changes could be as follows.

Change from: expecting your partner to be sensitive to your needs

Change to: self-care and acceptance of your partner's inability to meet your needs

Change from: an attitude that you have a right to tell your partner what to do, what not to do, and how do it

Change to: letting your partner do it her way, making requests and not demands, and accepting "no" as an answer without getting mad or sulking

Change from: expecting to be told the truth at all times

Change to: taking pains to verify in a discreet way

Change from: an attitude and expectation that your partner needs to change

Change to: accepting your partner as she is

Change from: expecting empathy, because you give empathy

Change to: restricting your openness to being empathic and realizing that your partner is unable to be empathic

You may want to explore for yourself what attitudes and expectations you have that, if changed even slightly, could produce positive outcomes for you. It could be something as simple as deciding not to confront your partner, thereby changing your attitude and expectation, and thus no longer telling your partner how they need to change.

Secure an Ally

You will find it beneficial to have someone in your immediate circle of family and friends or a therapist with whom to ally yourself. This is a person who can understand what you mean when you describe the troubling behavior and attitudes of your partner and their effects on you. This person is someone who has many of the following behaviors and attitudes:

• Does not try to talk you out of feeling the way you do.

- Does not try to "fix" it.

- Accepts the validity of your experiences.

- Does not demonize your partner in an attempt to support you.

- Is willing to listen and not tell you what you should or ought to do.

- Restricts giving advice, or gives none at all.

This ally can be a valuable resource for venting, talking out concerns, and getting emotional support. A major part of grounding strategies is to provide you with emotional support, and this person can help in a very constructive way.

What you want to avoid is someone who does the following:

- Criticizes you and your partner.

- Takes sides, instead of listening.

- Tries to tell you what to do or think.

- Minimizes the effect of your partner's behavior and attitudes on you.

- Attacks you or blames you for not changing your partner.

- Cannot understand what you are talking about or your position.

An ally can help you verbalize and work through your troubling feelings and is there to understand them with you.

Chapter 5

The Hungry Destructive Narcissistic Pattern

The descriptive categories for types of destructive narcissistic patterns are an attempt to be more specific about the different troubling patterns of behavior and attitudes. Categories can help you better understand your partner's needs, and they explain in part why your partner acts in a particular way. Chapters 5–8 present brief overviews designed to try to capture the essentials for each type. Read these with the awareness that no one person may exactly fit any type, that the categories are used as general guides, that you are reviewing these for a better understanding of your partner, and that you are not trying to manipulate your partner to change.

The Hungry DNP

People who can be described as having a hungry, needy, clinging, and dependent DNP are allowing their impoverished or "poor me" self to assume dominance. They tend to need excessive attention, but are grandiose at the same time. They can also switch very quickly between being hungry and being grandiose. Sometimes the switch is so rapid it happens as they speak the next word. This can put others at a definite disadvantage, as others can never know whether they are dealing with the hungry or the grandiose self, and even if they are correct, the Hungry DNP can switch again without notice.

Table 1: The Hungry DNP Scale

Directions: Rate your partner on the following items using the scale.
5—Always or almost always 4—Frequently 3—Sometimes 2—Seldom 1—Never or almost never

1. Seems to need considerable and constant attention	
2. Complains	
3. Looks to you to take care of his personal needs	
4. Pouts and sulks	
5. Is uncomfortable or anxious when you are unavailable	
6. Calls you from work to check in or chat	
7. Seems to expect to be disappointed	
8. Can be socially charming, but falls apart at home	
9. Is overly attentive to you	
10. Seems to want more than you are able to give	
11. Gets angry when left alone, seeks nurturing	
Total _____	

Scoring

Add your ratings. A score between 40–50 indicates a considerably Hungry DNP; a score between 30–39 indicates a very Hungry DNP; a score between 20–29 indicates a moderately Hungry DNP; and a score below 20 indicates little or no Hungry DNP. Let's examine the behavior and attitudes from the scale.

Considerable and Constant Attention

Does your partner seem to need considerable and constant attention, especially from you? Does your partner do and say things to keep your attention? Does your partner accuse you of paying more attention to someone or something than you do to him? Does your partner seem jealous of your friends, hobbies, or other outside interests? Do you feel you are dealing with a demanding child quite often? Whatever the attention, device, or means your partner uses, the goal is to keep your attention focused on your partner.

It is almost as if your partner fears that he will cease to exist or feels he only exists when he is the focus of attention. Actually, this can be a dominant, unconscious fear for people with a Hungry DNP. Attention is the way that these people can receive reassurance that their deep fear of abandonment, and/or destruction, will not come to pass, at least not for the moment. What you need to realize is that this deep-seated fear is unconscious, always present, and a considerable driving force for many behaviors and attitudes. As long as you or someone else gives the attention he craves and needs, the Hungry DNP feels confident that he exists. The final point is that he can never get enough attention to completely eliminate his fear.

Complains

Complaining is attention-seeking behavior and is also a way to signal that no one is taking care of his hunger. Some people who complain a lot think that they are telling others what's going on with them. They do not perceive it as complaining. To them, this is their way of connecting to you and letting you know how they feel. The partner with the DNP takes this to another level, because he expects you to "make it go away" or to fix it. His complaining is a way of connecting, but it is also a way of making his needs known.

However, many things he complains about are not things you can do anything about. They may be things that no one can do much of anything to resolve. Still, you may be left with feelings of incompetence and failure because you cannot resolve them and your partner criticizes, blames, or seems to blame you for that failure. If you were to point out that you lacked control or power to resolve whatever the complaint was about, your partner would immediately switch states and declare that you were trying to do something you were not qualified to do or would dismiss you in some way.

On the other hand, if the complaint resolution was under your power and control, and you took care of it, that would not make the complaining cease. Your partner would find something else to complain about. Or, you would not resolve it to their satisfaction and, once more, you would be blamed or criticized. You can become very wounded and self-critical because you are unable to resolve your partner's complaints.

Taking Care of Your Partner

Your partner may have high expectations that you will take care of his personal needs. What is expected is that you will fulfill many parenting and nurturing functions, so that your partner can remain free to pursue personally interesting things.

It can be difficult to separate the healthy caring and nurturing that takes place between partners from needs for caring and nurturing that are excessive. The intimate relationship demands a mutual caring and nurturing, although how each of you carries that out can and will be different. Caring and nurturing needs are excessive when many of the following are present:

- There is little or no mutuality or reciprocity of caring and nurturing.

- Your partner criticizes and blames you when he feels you fail to meet his needs.

- Many such needs remain unspoken by your partner.

- You are expected to read your partner's mind and provide what is needed.

- You are expected to do for your partner what he could easily do for himself.

- Your partner's demands and expectations never cease.

As soon as one thing is taken care of, another one pops up to take its place. Your partner seems very much like a whiney baby.

Your best strategy is not to challenge your partner, nor try to point out what your partner is doing. That will not work, and you may be accused of being insensitive and uncaring. You will have to make a personal decision about the extent to which you will meet your partner's expectations and demands. All of his expectations and demands are not unreasonable and can be considered a part of an intimate relationship. It is impossible for an outsider to say what is reasonable, what is unreasonable, or what is excessive.

A step you can take is not to chastise yourself for failure to read your partner's mind. Yes, you may be intuitive, or have experience knowing what your partner wants or needs, but you get it wrong often enough that there are still complaints. You can get out of the mind reading business and stop blaming yourself. You can say to your partner something like the following: "I'd like to be able to give you what you want, but you have to tell me what that is. I'm really not good at reading your mind, so I need you to be open with me and communicate your wants and needs." This may help the situation.

Pouts and Sulks

Hungry destructive narcissists use the childish tactics of pouting and sulking when dissatisfied or when they are thwarted from getting their way. This is a form of revenge, whereby you are supposed to understand that they have withdrawn their love and approval from you and will continue to hold out until you come around and become more satisfying and accommodating.

What is your response?

- Ignore your partner.

- Try to placate your partner.

- Start a fight, so that there will be some communication.

- Apologize for being unsatisfactory and unaccommodating.

- Retaliate in some way.

- Join in the pouting and sulking.

Unfortunately, some of the pouting and sulking occurs because you are not adept at mind reading; you have no idea what provoked the pouting and sulking. You don't know what you did or did not do that led to the pouting and sulking. And since your partner expects you to read his mind and know what you did or failed to do, your partner does not tell you, or openly refuses to tell you, what is bothering him. The more you try to find out, the further your partner retreats into pouting and sulking.

You may find it helpful to stop pursuing your partner to find the reason for the pout or sulk. When you do find out what it is, it will likely turn out to be a personal failure on your part and you will be further criticized and blamed. If you were feeling bad before you found out, you may very well feel worse after you find out what triggered the pout or sulk. It can be better to just let your partner have his mood.

It could also be helpful to act toward your partner as if he were not pouting or sulking. Continue to interact with him as if he were acting like an adult. Ignore the pouting or sulking, but don't treat your partner as if he does not exist.

Abandonment and Anxiety

This is a deep-seated fear that never goes away, but can be controlled. Your partner may manifest this fear by becoming very anxious when you are unavailable. This clinging behavior is experienced as attentiveness during the early stages of the relationship, but tends to intensify to the point where you can feel stifled and cut off from other relationships.

The items that refer to your availability, such as calling often to chat, can be reflections of this anxiety. Your partner fears that you will not be around to take care of him, and these are his ways of seeking reassurance. There are many ways the fear can be manifested and reassurance sought. The fear and need will continue to impact the person's behaviors and attitudes, until the person understands it and can take steps to manage and contain it. That takes a lot of personal self-exploration and can be facilitated by working with a competent therapist.

One of the most troubling outcomes of this fear is that this anxiety and need gets dumped on you, and when it is not met satisfactorily, you are blamed for not being good enough. It may be difficult for you to accept, but it is unlikely that you will ever be good enough to be completely satisfactory at meeting this deep-seated need. You may do the best you can, but find that your partner continues to feel anxious and needy, and that you are supposed to give him what is needed. These are impossible tasks and expectations.

Your major strategy will be to recognize and accept that your partner has this deep-seated fear and need and that neither you nor anyone else can do enough to eliminate them. Your partner is the only one who can learn to manage and contain the fear and need. Your recognition and acceptance of your limitation does not mean you should not try to meet any of your partner's needs. The relationship is important enough that you continue to give your partner as much as you feel you can without resentment, feeling overwhelmed, becoming enmeshed, or wanting to put some space between you. Your needs and feelings are also important. Try to give as much as you can, but stop at the point when you feel that what is being asked of you is an imposition.

Expects To Be Disappointed

The "poor me" part of a destructive narcissistic partner expects disappointment, and nothing ever quite measures up to the person's expectations, needs, wants, and desires. Embedded in this attitude is a profound hope for satisfaction that is never realized.

Also embedded in the poor me self is the notion that the self is not good enough, or else the hope would be realized. All this takes place on an unconscious level and is not accepted or acknowledged by the person. Your partner is unaware of these beliefs, feelings, and attitudes. All your partner knows is that others seem to be able to be satisfied, while he faces constant disappointment.

The grandiose self can successfully hide the poor me self and mask the deep disappointment experienced. This grandiose self will devalue and diminish others, remain dissatisfied regardless of efforts to please them, minimize the accomplishments of others, and assert their own superiority. Therefore, when you catch glimpses of the poor me self of your partner, you will find that the grandiose self is present, contemptuous, and/or dismissive of your efforts to help. Many times you will be left wondering what you did wrong when you were only trying to be helpful and supportive. The poor me self is thought to be shaming, as it can never be good enough. Thus, it must be hidden from the self and from others, although it remains an important part of the person's:

- self-perception,
- self-esteem,
- self-confidence,
- sense of self-efficacy,
- expectation of others,
- need for support and self-assurance,
- growth and development,

- underdeveloped narcissism, and
- attitude and behaviors.

Again, your best strategy will be to accept your partner "as is," and know that your partner is influenced by the poor me self in ways he does not know or understand, and that you are limited in your ability to do anything about it. You cannot make your partner satisfied. You can only try to make things less disappointing to the best of your ability and stop blaming yourself for not being able to keep your partner from being disappointed.

Charming but Falls Apart

Persons with Hungry DNPs can be socially adept and charming. They can be successful at work and function well in social situations. However, when they get home, they regress to a more childlike, dependent state; they fall apart. It's as if they can put on a suit of adultness for a period of time, but cannot maintain it or tolerate it as a part of their being.

Everyone can regress to a more childlike state and want someone to take care of them at some point. There is a cartoon that shows someone buried under a mound of debris yelling, "I want my Mommy," that resonates with many of us. However, this is a constant state for the Hungry destructive narcissist, and you, as their partner, are expected to fulfill that parenting and nurturing function. If you have wondered why your partner seems competent and able to take care of himself at work, but is very different at home, this description could be an answer.

It is helpful to understand that both personas are real. Your partner is both competent and needy. Your partner puts on the adult persona to satisfy the grandiose self and the childlike persona to satisfy the poor me self. Again, your partner remains unaware of doing this, and trying to make him aware is futile, so don't waste your time calling the switching to his attention.

Your understanding and acceptance can reduce some of the negative feelings you may have. Feelings that your partner leans on you too much, is too demanding, expects too much nurturing, or acts childishly can become a recognition that your partner feels helpless and is unaware of it. Your partner is helpless in the sense of being influenced by the poor me self and not knowing it. Until your partner becomes aware of it, he or she is not able to act or be any different.

Overly Attentive

Does your partner constantly seek reassurances from you by being overly attentive? You will have to define overly attentive for yourself, as it differs from person to person. The defining characteristics are many of the following.

- You have feelings of being smothered.

- The attention is often intrusive.

- You are reluctant to ask your partner to back off.

- Your partner feels hurt or rejected if you even hint at there being too much attention.

- Your partner wants you to share all your thoughts and feelings.

- You'd like an opportunity to do things for yourself or to be more independent.

The attention is not an indication of interest and caring under these circumstances, it is a means of power and control. You may even feel that you are back in the same situation you were in as an adolescent, when you were trying to convince your parents that you could handle independence.

It is difficult to manage your partner's behavior, as your being open and direct, or withdrawing, can arouse his anxiety, anger, or feelings of rejection. These actions signal that you are not willing to satisfy his need to take care of you, and that is very hurtful to your partner. The underlying reason, however, is not a need to take care of you, it is his deep-seated need for reassurance that you will not abandon him, either physically or psychologically. The slightest pulling away on your part can trigger these unconscious feelings and issues, and you can never provide enough of the needed assurance.

There are other considerations that impact your strategy for this behavior, such as your psychological boundaries, your collaborative behavior, and your personality. These are discussed in other sections. There is no particular strategy that you can use, except to be guided by understanding your needs, desires, and willingness to provide some constant reassurance to your partner. Understanding your partner's underlying need is a first step.

More Than You Can Give

This too is based on your feelings about what your partner is demanding of you, but you must be careful to get in touch with your underdeveloped aspects of narcissism to ensure that you are not projecting or off-loading your expectations on your partner. You will want to be sure that your partner is really being over-demanding and wanting more than you can give.

One way to get some objectivity is to reflect on the extent to which your partner seems to demand your attention, admiration, and services, but never gets enough, nor reciprocates. If there is some objective evidence or validation from other sources, then you are most likely correct in your perceptions. Others are able to see the clinging, dependent, and demanding behavior and attitude, even though they do not know some of the more intimate details. Further, it is hard to separate out unreasonable expectations and demands from those that are part of an intimate relationship.

If you feel your partner wants more than you can give, you are left to deal with your feelings of anger, frustration, guilt, shame, incompetence, and failure. These are your feelings, and these are what you will have to work on to reduce or eliminate. Your partner's need, behavior, and attitude are out of your power and control. You have to work on your self. The last chapter of this book can provide some guidance for a first step.

Other Behaviors and Attitudes

There are other behaviors and attitudes that can be exhibited by the person with a Hungry DNP, such as:

- hypersensitivity to any hint of perceived criticism,

- alertness to hints of potential devaluing of them,

- seeking gratification and verification of specialness from everyone,

- seducing of people who they feel can give them the nurturing and reassurance they crave, and

- easily enraged.

The poor me self contributes to many of these, as well as other behaviors and attitudes. The Hungry DNP expects rejection and pain, is fearful and vengeful, and is ever vigilant to protect the shameful, poor me self. The person with a Hungry DNP doesn't perceive this part of self. It is kept hidden from the self and others, but the person continues to act on its messages. No amount of attention, admiration, achievement, or acquisition of material goods can feed the impoverished part of self. Only the person with a Hungry DNP can become aware of the impoverishment and do considerable personal work to begin to fill this deep-seated and unconscious need.

Your Collaborative Behavior and Attitudes

There may be some behaviors and attitudes on your part that unconsciously support and encourage your partner's expectations, demands, and underdeveloped narcissism. You identified some of these in an earlier chapter, but there may be others that are especially important for you to understand as part of your relationship with a Hungry destructive narcissist.

Table 2:
Your Supportive Behavior and Attitudes

Directions: Rate yourself on the following items using the scale.	
5—Very much like you 4—Much like you 3—Somewhat like you 2—Little like you 1—Not like you at all	
1. Feel it is your responsibility to take care of others	
2. Feel guilty when others are uncomfortable	
3. Try to maintain harmony	
4. Put others' needs ahead of your own	
5. Get upset when you try to please someone, but are unsuccessful	
6. Work hard to please	

7. Are ready to sacrifice your best interests for others	
8. Try to read signals so that you can give others what they want or need before they ask	
9. Are alert to signs of distress from others	
10. Seek out ways to be helpful to others	
Total _____	

Scoring

Add your ratings. A scores of 40–50 indicates you have a considerable number of these collaborative behaviors and attitudes; 30–39 indicates that you have many; 20–29 indicates some; and a score below 20 indicates you have few or none.

Responsibility to Take Care of Others

This assumption is a valid one, as there is an interdependence for adults that fosters altruism, nurturing, and caring. It is a realization that one is not alone in the world and that relationships are strengthened when we assume this responsibility. However, if you do not recognize the limits of this responsibility, if you feel that you alone are responsible and must always "do something," then you are acting on an unrealistic assumption. You do have some responsibility, but you do not bear the entire responsibility to take care of others, especially when the other person is an adult. If you rated yourself 3+ on this item, you may be collaborating with your Hungry destructive narcissistic partner, who can easily trigger your feelings of guilt with just a hint that you failed in this responsibility. You may want to use some self-talk to remind yourself that your responsibility to take care of others is limited and that adults have some responsibility for self-care.

Others' Comfort

Do you feel that you are remiss in some way when others are uncomfortable? Do you rush to take care of them, so they will be comfortable? You may have internalized a parental message that you should take responsibility for other people's comfort, and that you are failing in some way if others are not comfortable. Thus, your feelings of guilt can be triggered when others appear to be uncomfortable.

Your partner can capitalize on this assumption and your feelings of guilt and can manipulate you to take care of them just by displaying some discomfort. You probably never stop to consider that your partner is a functioning adult who should be able to take care of his own discomfort under normal circumstances. This, of course, does not apply when your partner is ill or incapacitated.

Maintain Harmony

When you give in just to maintain harmony, you are doing yourself a disservice by subjugating your beliefs, values, principles, and even your best self-interest. You may have a fear of conflict, worrying that, if harmony is not preserved, you will be abandoned. This fear is unconscious and is probably tied to your family of origin experiences and issues. You may not even be aware of the terror you have that you will be left alone and cannot survive if that should happen.

It will take some time and effort to increase your level of comfort with conflict, and this should be gradual. Don't try to go from doing everything to maintain harmony to a stance where everything becomes a conflict. Instead, try reflecting on how you are compromising your beliefs, values, and principles in many situations with your partner in the interest of maintaining harmony. Some of these may not be worth changing your behavior to preserve, but some are. Pick a few to begin to stand up for and try to tolerate the anxiety it produces. Over time, you will be better at both of these— standing up and tolerating the anxiety.

Your Needs and Others' Needs

Every relationship can experience times and situations in which the other person's needs are of priority. The parent-child relationship is a prime example for when the other person's needs (the child's) are always a priority. But there are few adult-adult relationships where this is always true. If your partner can trigger your guilt and shameful feelings by suggesting that you are selfish when your partner's needs are not your priority, your partner can exploit and manipulate you.

Your guilt and shame can be a result of old parental messages, when you were expected to take care of your parents' needs, instead of the reverse. These messages, and the associated feelings for being remiss, have carried over to your other relationships and influence your current responses. This long-term and deep-seated condition can be difficult to overcome, but it can be addressed.

Trying to Please

Do you work hard to try to please others much of the time? How often are you successful at this? Do you feel that a part of your self-worth is dependent on the degree to which you are able to please someone, such as your partner? Are you under the impression that continually working to please others is altruistic on your part? If any or all of these fit you, then you are putting yourself in a position where your partner can easily manipulate you and where you cannot be successful. The Hungry destructive narcissist can never get enough or be filled up, and you can never please them. You cannot touch your partner's core need or yearning, and this failure can keep you busy trying to please without success.

You may want to explore why you have this need to please. Notice that this is termed a need, and not a simple desire. The usual or expected stance is that yes, we would like to please others and may even go out of our way sometimes to do this for some people. We feel disappointed when we are not successful. However, this behavior and attitude is a need, when it motivates you to keep working at it in the face of many failures *and* you feel you are flawed, unworthy, or shamed when you are unsuccessful. This need is deeper and has more intense feelings associated with it than what is found for the usual socialization attitude.

Sacrifice

When you sacrifice your best interests for someone, you do so with the hope that the sacrifice will be of benefit to the person, and when you are in need, there will be someone ready to do the same for you. Accompanying the sacrifice many times is also an expectation that the receiver will appreciate your efforts.

What is not so clear to you are your reasons for engaging in this sacrificing behavior. You probably never stop to ask yourself why this seems important for you to do. Nor do you understand how someone could fail to appreciate your efforts, since you were trying to be helpful to them. You may even be resentful that others are not always grateful. Some of this may be especially true for your partner, and you cannot understand your partner's responses and attitudes.

If you are often willing to sacrifice your best interests for others, you may be doing so:

- in an effort to control the other person by keeping them grateful and appreciative,

- to shore up your self-esteem and feel superior because of the sacrifice, or

- to manipulate that person.

There are other reasons for the willingness to sacrifice, but any of your unconscious reasons that lead to the behavior can be used by your destructive narcissistic partner to exploit you for their own ends. You may find that your partner' demands and needs call for a considerable amount of sacrificing of your best interests for them.

Reading Signals

Are you constantly alert to nonverbal signals that provide clues to what others want or need, in an effort to make sure you don't miss anything? Do you try to read others and anticipate their wishes? Is this behavior such a part of you that you are not fully aware of it? What could be happening is that you are continuing to act on familial expectations for you when you were a child, when you were punished or shamed for not reading these signals accurately or quickly enough. Although you are now an adult, you have transferred these messages, behaviors, and expectations to your other relationships.

An intimate relationship can allow each person to know and understand the other, to the extent that both can read nonverbal cues. You learn what each other's gestures, body positions, postures, voice tone, and other nonverbal communications mean, and there are times when you can anticipate your partner's wants or needs. This connection can be very comforting and valuable for the relationship. However, if you have to be constantly on edge and alert so that you anticipate your partner's needs and wishes in order to avoid his displeasure, you are collaborating with your partner's exploitive and manipulative behavior. You are not attending to your partner because you want to or for pleasure, you are doing so to avoid unpleasant consequences, such as abandonment. What you consider as unpleasant consequences, such as abandonment, guilt, and shame, can be a result of your long-term family of origin issues. These are best worked through with a competent therapist, as you are probably not fully aware of the reasons or of what you are doing. Some reading of your intimate partner is to be desired. Edgy and compelling reading of your partner's signals is not desirable.

Signs of Distress

The previous section also applies here, but is focused on distress, and carries an implication that you are alert to signs of distress because you feel you have an obligation to prevent, reduce, or eliminate the distress. This situation is similar to that of an attentive, or overattentive, parent and their children. Parents are expected to be able to read signs of distress in their children; however, in your situation, you are both adults, but one of you is cast, or has volunteered, to be in the role of an attentive parent. The Hungry destructive narcissist can benefit from this collaborative behavior, as he does not have to do anything about his distress, since your job is to fix whatever is causing the distress.

If you do tend to monitor your partner to be alert for his distress when your partner is not ill or incapacitated in some way, you may want to consider that you are assuming too much of a parental role, whereas you are supposed to be in an adult relationship. You are not your partner's mother or father, and you cannot fill the yearning or void your partner may have. Because you are a partner, you will want to take care of him as best you can, but you will want to do so as a partner, and not as a parent. You will want to convey confidence that your partner is capable of handling his own distress, just as you are capable of handling yours.

Being Helpful

The important point for this item is the part about seeking out ways to be helpful. In other words, you are not just helpful, you look for ways to be helpful. This behavior can signal some assumptions on your part that:

- you have an obligation to look for ways to be helpful,

- it is your responsibility to notice and to find ways to be helpful,

- you are remiss, and/or unworthy, if you don't look for and find these ways,

- others are relying on you and you must not disappoint them,

- you will feel guilty and shamed if you don't look for and find ways to be helpful, or

- your efforts will be appreciated and you will be valued.

Reaching out and being helpful to others is altruistic and commendable. This is one way to connect to others and to reduce alienation. Altruism is to be encouraged and applauded. But altruism is not what is meant here. What this item means and signals is that you are not content to be helpful when needed or requested. You actively look for what you think or feel needs to be done. You do not allow others to solve their own problems. You rush to provide assistance because of your need to be helpful. You are satisfying something within you or preventing uncomfortable feelings such as guilt or shame.

Your Hungry destructive narcissistic partner can capitalize on your feelings and assumptions and induce guilt and shame by even a suggestion that you did not do what you were supposed to do: that is, seek out ways to be helpful to him. You may want to try an experiment and wait for your help to be requested. You can announce that you are ready to help when asked, but that you will not help until you are asked. Allowing others to be independent and to take care of their own needs, but also providing the understanding that you are willing and able to provide assistance when requested, can be empowering.

How You Collaborate

You are probably wondering how your behaviors and attitudes contribute to supporting and encouraging your destructive narcissistic partner's troubling behaviors and attitudes. Be sure to read this section with the understanding that you are not being blamed for your partner. The intent is to make you aware that some of your assumptions about who you are and how you relate to others can assist and promote your triggered feelings, especially the more uncomfortable feelings. One hope for what is presented in this book is that you will learn to better understand, manage, reduce, or eliminate these feelings.

It would not be unusual for your guilt, shame, fear, or anger to get triggered in interactions with your partner. You may have tried to not let yourself become upset, but whatever you did was not effective and your partner was still able to get through to you. The previously described emotional insulation can be helpful to block your partner's projections, but you may still find that some uncomfortable feelings are aroused. These are the feelings that you produce, because of your self-perception. For example, if a basic self-perception of yours is that you are supposed to take care of others, then you can trigger your own feelings of guilt when your partner does or says something that indicates that you are failing to take care of them. The stronger this self-perception, the easier it is for your partner to charge you with failing to live up to your own self-perception, and the easier it is for you to trigger your feelings of guilt.

Review the items on the scale. Items you rated 3+ are the ones you are doing and holding as a self-perception to an extent that is collaborative; that is, you are holding these beyond the point that they are constructive and helpful for you. You are continuing to act on old parental messages about who you are, what you are expected to do and be, and how you are to relate to others. These are the behaviors and attitudes that support and encourage others' dependency, and dependency is the overall character of a Hungry destructive narcissist. Your tasks are to understand the behaviors and attitudes that foster dependency in others and to make needed changes. Examples of changes are as follows.

- Allowing others to take responsibility for their self-care.

- Understand that others contribute to their own discomfort and you do not bear any or all responsibility for their feelings.

- Become more comfortable with conflict and do not rushing to soothe or resolve it.

- Put your needs first when appropriate and accepting that there are times when that is appropriate.

- When you are unable to please someone, understand and accept that this person bears some responsibility and that you are not inadequate, nor are you not good enough.

- Become less concerned about pleasing others. Adults can take care of themselves. Except for when dealing with children, work to reduce the times when you are willing to sacrifice your best interests.

- Give others the space and responsibility for their self-care.

- Stop mind reading. Ask for what you want, and wait for others to let you know what they want or need.

- Reduce your alertness to signals of distress. Some distress is self-generated and self-corrective.

- Be ready to help, and recognize when help is needed, but do not go out of your way to look for ways to be helpful.

Chapter 6

The Suspicious Destructive Narcissistic Pattern

The category of Suspicious DNP describes people who are fearful of being hurt, rejected, and destroyed. They remain locked in their beliefs that others bear them ill will at all times, they must be ever vigilant and self-protective, and they cannot rely on support from anyone. Their world is a grim, uncomfortable one, where no one can ever be trusted. To get a feel for what their world is like, think of a police officer, an IRS agent, or a judge. These are occupations in which the commonly encountered behaviors are lies and misleading statements and information; where extensive steps are taken by many to cover up information and mistakes; and where the people in their professional roles are not liked and are devalued. Police officers, IRS agents, and judges have to develop a great deal of skepticism, cynicism, and mistrust of whatever they are told, no matter who it is telling them. This description is the mild version of the inner world of the person with a Suspicious DNP.

You cannot get really close to anyone with a destructive narcissistic pattern. But you can get closer to those with the other types than you can with someone who has a Suspicious DNP. This person was deeply hurt, rejected, and betrayed early in life, and other life experiences just reinforced the notion that to let people get close to you means that you will be hurt, rejected, and betrayed. You are trying to deal with a person who has had a lifetime of negative assaults on the core self. The best protection they have found is to keep their self away from others, to not allow others to get too close, and to always expect that others are seeking to hurt and destroy them.

There may also be a version of the poor me self with these people, as they may have a core assumption that if they were more worthy then others would not be trying to hurt and destroy them. This impoverished state is unconscious and must be hidden from others at all costs, since others would take any sign of weakness or inadequacy as evidence of their unworthiness or inferiority and use it to destroy them. These people work hard to keep others at a far distance, so that the impoverished self cannot be detected.

Rate your partner on the following items. Notice that the scale is very tentative. You are being asked to judge what someone else is thinking or feeling. Try to think as much as possible about what your partner says or does that gives you the impression that they think or feel a particular way. If your partner is Suspicious, it will be exhibited in words and deeds.

Table 1: Suspicious DNP Scale

Directions: Rate your partner on the following items using the scale.	
5—Always or almost always appears this way 4—Very often appears this way 3—Sometimes appears this way 2—Seldom appears this way 1—Never or almost never appears this way	
1. Says or does things to indicate she feels that others will take advantage of her	
2. Is hypersensitive to perceived criticism	
3. Can become jealous without provocation	
4. Is alert to potential threats to self-esteem	
5. Tends to devalue others and their motives	
6. Envies others perceived as not earning or deserving of achievements or possessions	

7. Can easily become argumentative	
8. Attacks others (on the offensive)	
9. Questions you in detail about many things	
10. Is skeptical and cynical	
Total _____	

Scoring

Add the ratings. A scores between 40–50 indicates considerable Suspicious DNP behavior and attitudes, a score between 30–39 indicates much suspicion; a scores between 20–29 indicates some suspicion; and a score below 20 indicates little or no suspicion.

Taking Advantage

Your partner may think that whatever anyone else does, their main goal is to take advantage of her in some way. She may not be clear as to what the advantage is or what is being done that gives her that impression, but she knows it is there. It doesn't help that she is correct many times in her life, as these experiences just reinforce her basic unconscious assumptions. In the instances where she is not correct in her perception that others are trying to take advantage of her, she considers this either an aberration or suspects that she just did not pick up on it.

This attitude also extends to you. Although you are closer to your partner than anyone else, you are also perceived as being poised to take advantage. This strongly ingrained attitude can be one of the reasons your partner asks so many questions, has to have considerable details, and becomes angry or hurt when you exhibit any reluctance to be interrogated. If you are not entirely forthcoming with extensive details or resist being questioned, your partner feels that you are hiding something and are doing so to gain an advantage.

You must realize and accept that the basic assumption that feeds her attitude is deep-seated and long lasting. You cannot be, explain, or do anything that addresses this attitude. You must also accept that your partner is unaware of the basic assumption as being deep-seated. She is convinced that the attitude is based on numerous life experiences and can quote you many events and situations to support the necessity of the attitude. It is also important to remember that there are people, in her world and in yours, who *are* seeking to take advantage.

Hypersensitive

Your partner may be deeply hurt or offended at any hint of perceived criticism, especially coming from you. This hypersensitivity is partly the grandiose self and partly the impoverished self. The grandiose self likes to think that the self is perfect, without flaws, and superior. The impoverished self feels flawed, shamed, and inferior. Both are unconscious states for the individual. The grandiose self acts to hide the impoverished state from being seen by the self or by others.

Thus, this person is always edgy and communicates this anxiety to others who are in their presence. You may find that you are tense, tentative in what you say, constrained in your communications with your partner, and frequently apologizing for offending. You know that you are not intentionally trying to hurt or offend your partner, but are unable to convince her of that, nor are you able to make any progress toward reducing or eliminating offensive and hurtful remarks.

You will never be able to significantly reduce or eliminate your partner's hypersensitivity and perception of criticism where none was intended. This too is deeply ingrained and unconscious for your partner, and you cannot effect a change all by yourself, no matter how well intended you are. Your partner may become less sensitive over time, but less sensitivity is not a whole lot less for this sort of hypersensitivity.

Jealous

Becoming easily jealous is another form that the fear of abandonment takes. When one is jealous, there is a fear that the desired or loved one will find others who are more attractive, worthy, and better in some way, and will leave to take up with that new person. The jealous person is anticipating and fearing loss of affection, caring, commitment, and validation as a lovable, worthwhile person.

The underlying assumption is, if I am good enough, my partner will prefer me over all others. The unconscious assumption is, I am flawed and not worthy, and so everyone will leave me for a better person.

Your partner may become jealous when your attention moves away from her to someone or something else. You may find that your partner objects, or becomes jealous, when you speak of someone else in a positive way. The Suspicious destructive narcissist sees abandonment at every turn and can be jealous of your family, friends, outside interests, pets, job, or time spent on hobbies.

In short, your partner wants your full attention and needs you to focus only on her. Your partner feels that less than your full attention means that you are poised to leave. This, of course, is not true for you, and you may find it difficult to understand or cope, as you don't know what is driving this jealous behavior. No amount of reassurance seems to be enough, and it never will. Your partner wants all your time, attention, and affection.

Potential Threats to Self-esteem

The Suspicious destructive narcissist has fragile self-esteem and can be easily narcissistically wounded. This means that inferences, comments, nonverbal gestures, meaningful looks, and almost anything can be viewed as a potential threat to the person's self-esteem. The impoverished part of self needs to be protected from hostile and destructive assaults by others. This is one of the reasons why the person with a Suspicious DNP will be contemptuous and dismissive of others. Destructive narcissists feel that their own flaws will be seen, and if others perceive these flaws, they will be contemptuous and dismissive in return. Thus, being perceived as flawed is very wounding. These people will take steps to counter any suggestion that they are less than perfect. This is the person who cannot or does not apologize, does not accept responsibility for errors and mistakes, is very critical of others, tries to show others in a "bad light," is quick to notice others' flaws and mistakes, and can be easily hurt by unintentional remarks and acts. Their reactions are an unconscious need to protect their fragile self-esteem. This, too, is deep-seated, and you will not be able to do or say anything that changes it.

Pointing out the ineffectiveness of their behavior will be counterproductive, as your partner will go on the offensive and accuse you of being insensitive and not understanding. You need your emotional insulation when your partner feels you are a threat to her self-esteem and mounts an offensive against you. You can make it a practice to: not agree with her depreciating comments about others, give up expecting apologies, ignore blaming and criticizing comments about you, and become self-monitoring when making comments about your partner to reduce the possible narcissistic wounding.

Tends to Devalue Others

This item is similar to the previous one about being alert to potential threats to self-esteem, which addresses the impoverished self. This item focuses on the grandiose self, where others are perceived as not good enough and your partner is perceived as superior. Both states can exist at the same time, or your partner can switch from one to the other in the blink of an eye.

You may find your partner tends to "put down" any and everyone, as not being right, good, or perfect. There is always some flaw. Your partner may give lip service to the notion of her own flaws, but does not really believe it. As long as she can see others' faults, she can feel superior, as she does not think she has the same faults. This is one way in which the grandiose self is manifested.

This attitude extends to what other people do, in that whatever they do is flawed, and this needs to be emphasized and highlighted. Suspicious destructive narcissists make their devaluing remarks with claims of wanting things to be better or perfect, but the real need is to show their superiority. What can be frustrating is that they can see minor flaws and focus on them as major ones. They don't see the good parts, or at least they don't comment on them. They are also adept at conveying an inference that you and others may be flawed, inadequate, and inferior to allow these flaws to exist. However, you must take care and not be so imprudent as to point out any of her flaws or mistakes. The need to protect the self is swift and intense, and your partner will go on the offensive.

Your best strategies are to use your emotional insulation and to build yourself to the point where you are accepting of your flaws and mistakes. You can admit to yourself and to others that you make mistakes without feeling wounded or inferior.

Envies Others

The notion that others are taking advantage contributes to the Suspicious destructive narcissist's envy. They feel that others have achieved because of some unfairness, as they are less worthy than and inferior to the destructive narcissist. Exactly what is envied is not important, it's the fact that the person has something that the destructive narcissist does not have, but feels is rightly theirs, and that that person does not deserve it. You may find that the Suspicious destructive narcissist envies others who:

- have status,

- receive awards,

- attain a promotion,

- excel in academic achievement or are better than they are,

- are considered good looking,

- have a family they consider to be better or superior,

- are wealthy, and

- get attention and admiration.

These examples show the wide range of things that can produce envy.

Because suspicious people assume conspiracies against them, your partner is convinced that everyone is working to prevent her from getting what is deserved. That may also include you. Her dissatisfaction with self can get displaced on you, and you are charged with not being good enough to make sure your partner gets what she deserves. Further, any of your achievements and successes are minimized, because of your partner's envy.

It does not help to point out to your partner how the other person worked for their achievement, nor to highlight the ways in which your partner has achieved and does not need to envy another person. She cannot accept that others can be superior to her in any way. Her envy is not amenable to rational discussion.

This is another characteristic about which you can do nothing, except to take steps to protect yourself and your family against your partner's potential excesses in her quest to have others envy her. She may not do anything except remain mired in misery and resentment. Some people, however, may begin to spend excessively, take financial and other risks, make unwise commitments, and do things to garner envy from others.

Can Become Argumentative

The need to protect the self from potential destruction is very strong for all with a DNP, but may be even stronger for Suspicious destructive narcissists. Their view of the world as a hostile and dangerous place filled with people who are bent on destroying them contributes to the strength of their responses to what is perceived as an attack or assault on the self.

They cannot tolerate a different point of view or opinion, and cannot see your asking a question as anything other than a challenge, criticism, put down, or an attempt to make them look or feel stupid. They cannot tolerate anything that differs from them in any way, for differences are an attack on the self. Some may fume in silence, but many become argumentative.

You may have expressed what you consider to be a mild difference of opinion with your partner, only to suddenly find that you are in a full-blown argument about something that is of no consequence, without understanding what happened. When this happens repeatedly, you can become cautious, tentative, or hold back expressing your perception and opinions just to avoid arguments. You have found that you cannot win or prevent these arguments. The bad news is that you are correct. Any or all differences are threatening to your partner and will produce discord. Your partner must protect herself, does not realize what she is doing, nor why, is not open to exploring or discussing her reactions, and sees no reason to change. Change can only happen when your partner is ready to make changes for herself.

Goes on the Offensive

All attacks are not arguments. When your partner feels the self is in danger, attacks can take the form of:

- sarcasm,

- devaluing comments,

- criticism and blame,

- taunting,

- put downs,

- ignoring you, and

- deliberate acts designed to irritate or hurt.

In short, your partner exacts revenge for what she perceives as a deliberate attempt on your part to hurt and destroy her core self. Some retaliatory acts are passive, such as ignoring you, but are still offensive acts.

These attacks can be hard to cope with and can erode your self-esteem and the relationship. You may also be unaware of what you do or say that triggers the attacks. You may have even examined past events for clues, trying to prevent attacks by using that information as a guide for what not to do or say, but find that the attacks still continue. You do not want to offend your partner, but haven't been able to manage that so far.

A troubling outcome for you is the distressing and uncomfortable feelings you experience during and after these attacks. You are likely to experience anger, fear, guilt, and shame, to mention a few. These feelings are likely to be intense and long lasting, and you would like them to stop. This is another situation where your emotional insulation can help. You cannot prevent the attacks, but you can protect yourself. Another possible strategy is to refuse to join in the attacks by not becoming angry or defensive and by not even trying to explain what you mean or don't mean. Apologize when absolutely necessary and, unless your partner says openly that her feelings are hurt, do not assume that you are at fault for hurting her feelings. You usually wind up feeling worse when you do. If you did offend, content yourself with saying something like, "It was not my intent to hurt or offend, and I'm sorry that what I said or did had that effect on you." Try to stop beating yourself up over her hurt feelings. The reason for her hurt is unconscious, deep, and long-standing. You cannot address it, and it is more helpful to stay focused on your intent and to take care of your triggered feelings.

Questions in Detail

Some people, in their desire to understand something, will ask numerous questions to learn many details about whatever it is.

Some people, on both the receiving and sending ends, view this as a sign of interest, while some, on the receiving end, view the questioning as attacks. You may be one of the latter and may have a strong resistance to being questioned in detail.

The person who has a Suspicious DNP uses questions to intimidate, to exert power and control, and to verify their conviction that you and everybody else is trying to hurt and destroy her. And, as a means of putting you on the defensive, she keeps you emotionally upset and unable to remain rational and objective, she highlights your errors and mistakes, and she shows her superiority and your inferiority. She has numerous unconscious reasons for these behaviors.

In addition, your partner can exaggerate anything that she considers to be inconsistent, irrational, or resistant. She can be quick to describe you as being secretive, keeping her out, not wanting her to be an integral part of your life, or lying. If you hesitate at all when responding, she jumps on that hesitation as evidence that you are not being forthcoming and telling the truth. On the other hand, if you answer very quickly, she is also suspicious.

You are the best judge of your willingness to be questioned in detail. It may be an irritation at some times and a major annoyance at others, but you don't consider it a big deal. Or you may become really angry when bombarded with questions. Whatever your response, the one strategy that will help is to use your emotional insulation, so that your negative feelings are not aroused. You can exhibit calmness, indifference, or a desire to provide the information.

Skeptical and Cynical

These characteristics seem to develop over time with experiences that promote them for some people. That is, they have enough experiences whose outcomes make them cautious, questioning, or slow to trust or believe, and they have to be convinced before participation or commitment. It can be prudent for adults to look before they leap, operate on the notion that if it sounds too good to be true, it probably isn't true, suspect that the check is not in the mail, or believe that "this is for your own good." However, Suspicious destructive narcissists carry this attitude and perspective to an extreme and are skeptical about everyone and everything.

Skeptics and cynics expect the worst and are usually not disappointed. When the outcome is positive, they remain unconvinced that something negative is not lurking or hidden. If this description fits your partner, she cannot enjoy much of anything. Your partner is guarded, alert to possible negative consequences and outcomes, continuously challenging of almost everything, and makes no secret of her feelings by making negative comments.

If you are dealing with these attitudes and behavior by trying to point out the positive, disagreeing about the negative, or in some way trying to get your partner to change her attitude or perspective, you need to stop. What is likely happening is that you are strengthening her mistrust, giving her cause to feel that you are critical and not supportive of her, and that you do not value her. While none of these are your intent, it still does not prevent your partner's feelings. Worse, your partner is correct many times when being skeptical and cynical, and revels in pointing out to you that she was correct. When this happens, your negative feelings can be triggered.

Keep your perspective and allow your partner to keep hers. Don't try to talk your partner into being more positive and less negative, as that will not work and can make her even more skeptical and cynical. She has sufficient evidence that her attitude is correct and realistic.

Your Collaboration

Your collaborative attitudes and behaviors, as well as some of your assumptions, beliefs, and actions, can contribute to your partner's behaviors and attitudes that are negatively impacting you. You are not contributing to their DNP, as that was developed from birth on. But you may be thinking, doing, and feeling things that intensify your partner's negative impact on you.

Table 2: Collaborating with the Suspicious DNP Scale

Directions: Rate the extent to which you do, think, or feel each of the following using the scale.

5—Always or almost always
4—Often
3—Sometimes
2—Seldom
1—Never or almost never

1. Agree with her devaluing remarks	
2. Blame others for your distress	
3. Are sensitive to criticism	
4. Are easily hurt by your partner's remarks	
5. Do things so that others will like you	
6. Crave nurturing and attention	
7. Become defensive and try to explain when challenged, criticized, or confronted	
8. Think that you are not appreciated	
9. Feel guilty for not being a better person	
10. Engage in flirtatious and seductive behavior to get your partner's attention	
Total _____	

Scoring

Add your ratings. A scores between 40–50 indicates that you have a considerable number of actions, thoughts, and feelings that are supportive of your partner's Suspicious DNP; a score between 30–39 indicates many of these; a score between 20–29 indicates some of these; and a score below 20 indicates a few or none.

Agreeing with Devaluation

If you verbally agree with your partner when she does any or all of the following, you are agreeing with your partner's devaluing remarks.

- Makes disparaging remarks about you.

- Puts you down.

- Finds fault and is picky about many things you do.

- Constantly points out how you can improve.

- Criticizes your physical self.

- Cannot be satisfied with anything less than perfection from you.

It can be helpful for you to refrain from openly agreeing with these devaluing comments, even if, or when, they have an element of truth in them. You can accept personal responsibility without accepting or agreeing with the devaluing remarks. Another strategy to accompany the previous one is to not take offense and become visibly upset. You deflate her sense of superiority and self-importance when you fail to respond in a negative way to her negative comments. Yes, they do mean the devaluing comments personally, but you do not have to take them personally.

There are some things you do *not* want to do.

- Go on the offensive and attack your partner.

- Become visibly hurt or upset.

- Deny the validity of the remark that has a truth component.

- Point out a fault that your partner has.

- Sulk or pout.

- Angrily leave or withdraw.

These are responses that can make a bad matter worse.

Blame Others

If you rated yourself 3 or higher on this item, you are contributing to your own distress and you are failing to take personal responsibility for your feelings. Others do not make you feel a particular feeling, you choose to feel the way you do. For example, what others do or say does not make you feel guilty or ashamed. What happens is that the person does or says something that arouses old parental messages, cultural and societal expectations, or personal values that you associate with your failure to live up to expectations, or that reminds you of what you consider to be a personal flaw. Then your guilt or shame is triggered. The other person did not cause or make you have the feeling in the sense that they are powerful enough to control your feelings.

Your destructive narcissistic partner can use this characteristic of yours to her advantage by intensifying your anger, defensiveness, guilt, and shame. She accomplishes this by criticizing you for blaming others, instead of accepting your personal responsibility. Even when you are correct and whatever happened is not your fault, your partner can arouse these feelings. They can be triggered because you may start to wonder if any part of it was your responsibility. You may have to do a lot of explaining to convince your partner that you are not just using your usual response of blaming others.

You will find it helpful to accept your personal responsibility and its limits. You are responsible for some things sometimes, but not everything all of the time. There are times when you do bear some responsibility for what happens, and there are times when you have little or no responsibility. Your need to be blameless could be profitably explored with a competent therapist, as the need is unconscious and related to something deep-seated. An adult response is to accept your responsibility, but not to accept blame when you're not responsible.

Sensitive to Criticism

You may be so sensitive to criticism that you jump to respond defensively whenever your partner criticizes you. Sad to say, but you will never find a way to prevent or eliminate your partner's criticizing remarks. No matter what you do, changes you make or attempt to make will make her aware of the hurt you experience when criticized. Your partner will continue to make these criticizing remarks. Your reactions only contribute to your distress.

Instead of trying to get your partner to stop criticizing you, you may find it more helpful to explore your reactions and make changes there. Building your self can help you be less sensitive and hurt when criticized. Exploring and building self can take place in a variety of ways, including therapy. Understanding yourself is a first step.

The benefits of working on yourself are many, such as the followi.ng

- Having a fortified and secure self.

- Having a better grounded and centered self.

- Reducing or eliminating your sense of being overwhelmed or enmeshed by others' feelings.

- Warding off projective identification.

- Becoming more appropriately empathic.

- Experiencing less fear of abandonment and destruction of self.

- Exerting more control over distressing feelings, like shame, guilt, anger, and fear.

This is the kind of work that will allow you to use any criticism in a constructive way, ignore unhelpful criticism, and lessen the hurtful impact of these remarks on you. You will learn how to not perceive and react to criticism as if it is pointing out your shameful character flaws.

Easily Hurt

You can be hurt, feel rejected, and be made ashamed by the demeaning and devaluing remarks of your partner. These comments are calculated to emphasize how you are failing to be what is desired, and the extent to which you are inferior and not good enough. Your self-confidence, self-esteem, and self-efficacy can be eroded, and you begin to experience considerable doubt.

If you find that you are easily hurt, and these feelings linger long after the event is over, you may want to approach the concern from the following perspectives and fronts. The first is the external, where you can employ your emotional insulation so that the hurtful intents can be screened out. The second approach is cognitive, in that you can consciously decide not to react to the comments in a defensive way. You can do the following:

- Not allow your hurt to be seen.

- Not take the comments personally.

- Focus on your strength and think or make self-affirming statements to yourself.

- Interrupt any personal slides into rejection and hurt.

In short, you must think, instead of feel, or at least most of your conscious focus must be on thoughts. The third approach is to work on the personal issues that still linger from your family of origin. The most constructive strategy is to use all of these.

Trying To Be Liked

Your deep need to be liked can be playing into your Suspicious destructive narcissistic partner's hands, because you will do almost anything to ensure that you remain in her good graces. You fear abandonment and destruction if you are not liked, because you have a conviction that liking is equated with nurturing and safety. Not being cared for and safe leads to destruction.

Another side of this is that you are looking outside yourself for this nurturing and safety. You also have the conviction or assumption that you cannot adequately provide for yourself, and that others are necessary for your survival. Thus, in order to survive, you will do whatever is needed to get others to take care of you and keep you safe. Others must like you so that they will be willing to assume this responsibility.

This stance, conviction, or assumption can lead you to do things that are contrary to your values, beliefs, principles, and moral and ethical standards in the quest to gain or keep others liking you. Your partner capitalizes on your need to be liked and can exploit you to meet her needs. Much of this takes place on an unconscious level, and you are able to recognize what happened only in retrospect. You seldom, if ever, connect your need to be liked with the ease with which you can be exploited or manipulated to do things you do not wish to do.

To overcome, reduce, or eliminate your need to be liked will take a lot of effort and time working on your personal development. The old parental messages, family of origin experiences, and your basic personality combine and operate in complex ways to produce this deep-seated need. You can benefit from having a better understanding of yourself, building stronger and more resilient boundaries, and working through unresolved issues. This is a long-term process and much patience is needed.

For the short term, you may want to try to use some self-talk to prevent you from doing things you do not wish to do. Self-talk means having a conversation with yourself in which you are saying things like:

- "I can survive without this person's approval and liking."

- "If this person likes me, it does not mean they will care for me and keep me safe."

- "If this person does not like me, it does not mean I am not worthwhile and will not survive."

- "I am able to care for myself and keep myself safe."

- "I do not have to do things I don't want to just to please someone else."

Crave Nurturing and Attention

How much do you want, need, yearn for, and crave nurturing and attention? What is meant here is that you have a deep and intense desire for being nurtured and getting attention. This deep and intense desire is more than the usual need that is expected in an intimate relationship. It is overwhelming and consuming, and can be a major contributor to your distress. This is especially true if the description also fits you in relationships other than with your partner.

Just like the underlying assumptions and convictions described for the previous item, this one also is tied to a deep-seated need for reassurance that you will be taken care of so that you will survive. This need is something you hold in common with your Suspicious destructive narcissistic partner, whereby she too craves nurturing and attention as a means of assuring survival.

If you are honest enough to admit your deep desire for nurturing and attention, you are well on your way to doing something to change, so that you will not be easily exploited or manipulated via your craving. This will take a lot of personal work. Another step you can take in the short term is to examine your past and present actions to see which were reflective of your craving, if the craving was satisfied or not, and if you were manipulated or exploited. You can decide if the outcomes of your actions were sufficiently positive for you.

Understanding your craving can certainly help you to make changes you consider necessary. The self-reflection described previously can also be helpful. Staying in touch with your craving, and questioning its inference when you are faced with doing something someone else wants you to do, can also be of assistance.

Defensive Behavior

In *Webster's II New College Dictionary* (1999), the core meaning of defend is "to keep safe from danger, attack or harm;" the fourth definition for defense is "an argument in support or justification." These definitions are presented so that you can get an understanding of why you are considered as being defensive when you think you are explaining your position. Many, or most, people perceive an explanation as a protective device that is used because you feel threatened. You may not feel threatened, but that is what the other person is thinking. This perception is why you may be taken aback when your partner tells you to "not be defensive" when you try to explain what you mean, your opinion, or your perspective. If you do tend to explain because you want others to understand, then you may want to try to reduce or eliminate this practice. Try this not only for interactions with your partner, but also with other people. Whether or not others openly express that they think you are being defensive, many do think so.

When you are perceived as feeling threatened, you can be thought of as:

- weak,
- irrational,
- timid,
- overreacting, or
- fearful.

In fact, you may be feeling none of these, but are reacted to as if you were. These are some very good reasons to stop the practice.

You will not, most likely, be comfortable when you first begin the practice of not explaining. You must also be prepared for others to be surprised, and some people, including your partner, may not react very well. However, if you persist, you will become more comfortable and others will stop having negative perceptions of you as being defensive. If someone wants an explanation, let that person request it. Just wait until you are asked for more information instead of rushing to provide it.

You Are Not Appreciated

When you have the persistent thought or idea that you are not appreciated, you can become resentful, bitter, withdrawn, aggressive, or have other negative reactions. You may sulk, pout, become argumentative, whine, or do other things that grate on people's nerves and that push them away. Your attempts to get what you want and what you feel you deserve do not seem to work. Further, your reactions and behavior provide more opportunities for your partner to criticize you. This leads to guilt and shame, as you realize that there is some validity to the criticism. All in all, you are not comfortable with your self, nor are others comfortable with you.

Everyone wants their efforts to be appreciated, but we all differ in the need to have visible signs of this appreciation. Some people are content with self-satisfaction, while others cannot be satisfied unless there is strong and consistent external appreciation expressed. Those are the two extremes and everyone is somewhere on a continuum between the two.

An additional complexity is that you may be correct—you may not be appreciated. However, the important point is how you react and behave, not the validity of your perception. If you have a strong need for visible signs of appreciation, you will feel hurt and rejected whenever you do not receive them, and there will be numerous opportunities for this to happen. Your challenge will be to reduce the intensity of this need of yours, so that you seek visible signs of appreciation less and are less wounded by their absence. Becoming less wounded and lessening the intensity of your hurt and rejection can allow you to reduce the instances where you can be criticized by your partner. You can also develop and fortify your self to become more self-appreciative, that is, more confident and accepting that you and your efforts are good enough. In short, you do not have to continue to think you are or feel unappreciated.

Not Good Enough

Feeling guilty for not being a better person needs some self-examination to determine if this guilt is induced by others, such as your partner, or if it is aroused because you are not living up to personal standards. If the first is true, you are reacting to a projective identification or are having old parental messages triggered. If you feel guilty because you are not living up to your personal standards, this too can stand some self-examination to determine if you still choose these standards, or if you continue to feel and act on them because you've always had them.

Almost everyone can experience guilt at not being a better person sometime during their life. This guilt can help in self-development, as an impetus for atonement and behavior change. This is a constructive use of guilty feelings. However, if your personal principles and standards were incorporated by you without thought or examination, then you may be feeling guilty because of old parental messages, cultural expectations, religious teachings, and other external influences in your early life. These still may be acceptable and suitable for you as an adult, but they should be revisited, examined, and freely chosen now that you are an adult.

When guilt can be induced by your partner for your not being a better person, you can be the target of a projective identification, whereby your partner projected her feelings about not being a better person onto you, you accepted these feelings, identified with all or part of them, and triggered your guilt, or you acted on your partner's projected guilt. Your level and extent of self-knowledge and self-understanding determine if your feelings of guilt are all yours, or are a part of your acting out a projected feeling. Either way, you are feeling guilty at not being a better person.

The distinction can be an important one for deciding on a strategy. If you are acting on an unexamined part of self, unconscious identifications from your parents, and cultural expectations, your strategy will be to engage in self-reflection on your values, assumptions, principles, and beliefs. There may be room for self-improvement, and your desire to stop feeling guilty about not being good enough can lead to positive changes. On the other hand, if your guilt is induced by projective identification, you can use your emotional insulation to keep the projections out and thwart your identifying with the projection. You may want to consider doing both described strategies, because understanding your unconscious assumptions about being a better person can lead to less identification when a projection does manage to get through your emotional insulation.

Finally, it will take time to do the above. Be patient with yourself and use some self-talk when feeling guilty about not being a better person. Practice self-talk that reminds you to engage in self-reflection, to make positive changes, and to remember to use your emotional insulation.

Flirtatious Behavior

Do you engage in flirtatious and/or seductive behaviors? Are you doing so to get your partner's attention? If your partner has a Suspicious DNP, you are fueling their fears of abandonment. Your behavior may seem harmless to you, but whatever the intent, it does not feel harmless to your partner. You get her attention, but you also reinforce her deep fear.

It could be helpful for you to explore your need for your partner's attention and why you are using this indirect way to try to get it. After all, there are other and more constructive ways to get her attention. You may also want to explore what is going on that makes you feel that your partner is not attending to you. Notice that the focus is on what is causing you to feel as you do, and not on what your partner is doing or not doing. Keep your focus on your feelings.

Your Suspicious destructive narcissistic partner is already convinced that it is dangerous for her to trust anyone, and when you engage in behavior that can signal potential abandonment, you intensify that conviction. However, your partner's attention on you to keep you from abandoning them will not necessarily be positive for you. It does not make any difference to your partner that you are:

- not rejecting them,
- not intending to leave,
- not saying that your partner is inadequate,
- not really interested in the other person, or
- just seeking their attention.

Your partner will act on her deep fear and lack of trust. Your best strategy is to cease these behaviors and do some self-examination.

Chapter 7

The Manipulative Destructive Narcissistic Pattern

Relationships with Manipulative destructive narcissists can be a real emotional roller coaster. You are up, down, around, and stopped throughout the whole experience, and sometimes in a single inter-action with them. You are living in a very ambiguous, unstable, and upsetting situation, as this person thinks that he or she:

- is superior to others,

- has a right to exploit anyone and everyone,

- is only doing what everyone else does, and knowingly lies, distorts, and misleads,

- is entitled to be contemptuous,

- keeps him/herself in a spotlight by boasting and bragging,

- can get personal needs met by telling others what they want to hear, and

- can get others to do his/her bidding by being charming and seductive.

You never know which state is being presented at any time, until some time later. Sometimes, or within nanoseconds, the inflated self is what your partner presents to you, by boasting and bragging, but then switches to the poor me state, by cajoling you to do something you do not want to do. It is very disconcerting to experience a switch of these states during an interaction, and that is frequently what happens.

But before we go any further in the description of a person with a Manipulative DNP, let's determine if your partner has behaviors and attitudes associated with this DNP.

Table 1: Manipulative DNP Scale

Directions: Rate your partner on the following items using the scale.	
5—Always or almost always 4—Often or very often 3—Sometimes 2—Seldom 1—Never or almost never	
1. Easily lies, cheats, distorts, and misleads	
2. Enjoys "putting something over" on others	
3. Feels entitled to take advantage of others	
4. Doesn't appear to feel guilty when caught lying	
5. Is adept at off-loading blame	
6. Feels superior	
7. Is contemptuous of others	
8. Boasts and brags	
9. Engages in seductive behavior	
10. Seeks to arouse envy in others	
Total _____	

Scoring

Add your ratings. A score between 40–50 indicates considerable Manipulative DNP of behaviors and attitudes; a score between

30–39 indicates much manipulation; a score between 20–29 indicates some manipulation; and a score below 20 indicates little or no manipulation.

Cheats, Lies, Distorts, and Misleads

Have you ever observed small children at play, making up rules that favor them, and making them up as they go along? Children will sometimes do whatever it takes to win or to get what they want, and this is typical behavior for childhood. Adults, on the other hand, are expected to know and observe the rules, play fair, and not cheat or lie. Adults are supposed to be more mature than children, but as you know from your personal experiences, this is not always the case.

People with destructive narcissism have their personal needs as a top priority at all times. They are considerably self-absorbed, cannot imagine being any other way, and are convinced that everyone else is just as they are. Thus, it is easy for them to engage in this sort of behavior and have these attitudes. They are only doing and feeling what they assume that others are doing and feeling.

If you are in a relationship with a Manipulative destructive narcissist, you have encountered your partner's cheating, lying, distorting, and misleading. Your partner sees nothing wrong with these behaviors and attitudes, and is not about to change. Your confrontations and challenges do not work. You may be at the point where you are very frustrated, don't know what to believe or expect, and are at a loss to know what to do about it. Talking out your concerns with your partner does not work.

You really need to come to terms with the reality of your relationship and your partner's behaviors and attitudes. Your partner is unlikely to change. That is a hard concept to acknowledge and accept, but it is the reality. Your partner will have to initiate the desire to change and work hard with a therapist to effect significant changes, and none of these are within your power or under your control.

You probably become deeply disappointed each time you are faced with your partner's cheating, lying, distorting, and misleading. There may also be some frustration, anger, dismay, and hurt that your partner would treat you this way. However, these are your responses, and these you can work to change. Your best strategy is to do what was just described: accept the fact that your partner will do whatever she feels will achieve her need or goal; understand that many or most times what your partner is doing or saying is not exactly the truth and needs verification; and work to reduce your distressing feelings.

"Putting Something Over"

Pulling the wool over someone's eyes and putting something over on someone describe the behaviors of conniving, manipulative, destructive narcissists. These people are dedicated to taking advantage of others in any way possible in their search for reassurance of their superiority. They revel in their successes and can become very angry and hurt if you suggest that there is anything wrong in the tactics they use to achieve their goals. They, of course, can do no wrong, and if they use what you are terming as unfair tactics, it is only because that is what everyone else is doing, and therefore they are justified in using these tactics.

This attitude also extends to you. Your partner may enjoy putting something over on you and take great pleasure in describing the shortcomings that allowed this to happen to you. She may tell you, if you were smarter, more alert, or more worthy, you could have prevented this from happening. The real situation is that nothing you do or use will prevent your partner from succeeding at this. You are not able to change her attitude, nor are you able to stop or prevent your partner from trying to put something over on you.

Your partner's inflated self and need for reassurance of superiority demand that she use every opportunity to shore up her superiority by highlighting and emphasizing others' inferiority. Her superiority is only supported where she can show that others are:

- inadequate,

- incompetent,

- less intelligent,

- stupid,

- ignorant, and

- less worthy.

If your partner truly felt superior, there would be no need to have others as inferior in order for her to feel superior.

Unless you want to spend all or a considerable amount of your time thwarting your partner's efforts to put something over on you, you cannot win in this situation. You would have to be constantly alert, read ambiguous signals, gather a lot of useless information, and be ready to spring into action, but would still be unable to forestall or eliminate having something put over on you. It is not worth the time and effort that it would take.

Your best strategy is to understand that this need is really a cry for reassurance and that your partner will never receive sufficient reassurance to stop this behavior. Don't comfort, chide, or try to show your partner another perspective. These behaviors just reinforce her need for reassurance. Your partner receives reinforcement for the attitude and behavior from being correct that someone *is* trying to take advantage in many instances. It isn't easy to accept, but you are unlikely to make a difference. The best you can do is to protect yourself from any negative feelings that you may experience when your partner puts something over on you.

Entitled To Take Advantage

The description of a con man or woman illustrates this attitude. Con people are charming and seductive in winning others' confidence with the goal of swindling or duping them for the con person's gain. They refer to their targets as pigeons, dupes, marks, and other terms that are designed to show the target's inferiority and to reinforce the notion that others are to be taken advantage of and don't deserve what they have. An associated notion is that, if these people were worthy, they would not be in a position where someone could take advantage.

This entitlement attitude points out the lack of empathy and altruistic feelings that people with a DNP can have. They simply cannot put themselves in others' shoes, nor do they feel they have any obligation to look out for or to care for others. They are responding to a deep conviction derived from their infant and childhood experiences, in which their emotional and psychological needs were not met.

The entitlement attitude is accompanied by an inflated self whose superiority is to be maintained at all costs, and others must recognize this. Failure to do so brings revenge, disdain, and other retaliatory acts. It is not safe to let these people know that you do not perceive yourself as inferior or them as superior.

If your partner exhibits this attitude, you need to be aware that you are perceived by her as there to be used, exploited, and taken advantage of, without protest on your part. She feels entitled to do these things and you are expected to recognize and accept her right. Another piece of this is that she is also likely to unconsciously consider you as an extension of herself, and thus under her control. It's like she sees you as a different person, but doesn't really understand the concept to the point where you can be accepted as acting on your personal needs or desires—you are expected to fulfill hers.

Again, you must accept that this attitude is deep-seated, long lasting, and associated with early life experiences. These are not easy to change, even when the person works with a competent therapist, and you are not likely to be able to do, say, or be anything that will change your partner. You can only learn to protect yourself and, if you have children, to protect them. Your best personal protection will be strong and resilient psychological boundaries.

Doesn't Appear Guilty when Caught

Most people who have internalized the parental and cultural value that lying is not acceptable will feel guilt when caught in a lie. Some may feel guilty when lying even if no one catches them. However, many with a Manipulative DNP will not appear to feel guilt when caught in a lie. They seem to shrug off what would produce guilt and shame for many other people.

It cannot be said with any assurance that they do not feel guilt. This is beyond our knowing, and if the person is adept at lying, we can never know if their saying they feel guilt is truthful or not. What we can be is aware of the appearance of feeling guilty.

Why even mention this? After all, you know what it is like to feel guilty and you most likely would rather not have the experience. It isn't pleasant to feel that you have failed to live up to or act in accord with:

- your personal values,
- society's expectations,
- parental teachings,
- ethical and moral standards.

Having to pay attention to what you should or ought to say or do can be limiting and produce frustration, and that is something you would give up if it were possible to do so. However, for you, it is not possible. Another aspect is that you can have an assumption that other people, including your partner, operate from the same or a similar internalized state, where guilt is felt for transgressions such as lying. It can be a shock to realize that someone does not experience guilt when caught lying.

The lack of guilt feelings can also allow your partner to go on the offensive when caught in a lie or when challenged for lying. You may have experienced something like this, where you tried to confront your partner about a lie or about the practice of lying, only to have her mount an attack on you, with the result that you end up with all the unpleasant feelings. Learn this lesson and do not confront. If your partner does not appear to feel guilty when caught in a lie, leave it alone. You cannot help your partner, yourself, or the relationship by confronting or challenging. All you can really do is to deal with the personal feelings that may arise because it does not seem to bother your partner to lie.

Off-loading Blame

If your partner has a Manipulative DNP, you are likely to be accustomed to her tendency to off-load blame, and many times you are the recipient of the blame. It doesn't matter how big or small the offense is, your partner never accepts responsibility for mistakes as errors. Worse, you may be blamed for things that are not your fault or are not under your control.

This tendency to off-load blame is a manifestation of the inflated self. Your partner feels that she can do no wrong and is superior. Other words to describe this self-perception and attitude are grandiose and omnipotent. Just think of a toddler who breaks something. The toddler will deny breaking it and explain that an imagined person or being broke it. Children are also expert at blaming each other, pets, ghosts, you name it, in the effort to off-load blame. This behavior is understandable at an early age, but is less understandable when exhibited by an adult.

Manipulative destructive narcissists have become proficient at off-loading blame, as the self cannot be anything less than perfect. There are times when their protests seem to have some validity, and this can keep you off-balance to the point where you don't know what to believe. Your partner doesn't care about validity or anyone else. She is only interested in being blameless.

This stance is a defense against feeling:

- guilt,

- shame,

- less than perfect,

- that others are better or superior,

- less able, competent, or intelligent,

- the inability to be effective, and

- self-doubt.

These are all threats to the inflated self and must be warded off at all costs. You may even find that your partner is willing to off-load the blame on a child, rather than having to admit personal responsibility.

If this description fits your partner, there are some strategies that you can use. The first is to stop any practice of trying to establish who is at fault. That is very threatening to someone with a Manipulative DNP and will trigger their defenses in an instant. Don't worry about who is to blame or about having them admit blame—just fix whatever it is and move on. You'll save wear and tear on your nerves if you can do this.

The second strategy is to fortify your psychological boundaries, so that you do not accept the off-loaded blame when you do not deserve it. You can limit your triggered feelings of guilt and shame when you do not unconsciously identify with unconscious projections from your partner. Building your psychological boundaries will allow you to accept personal responsibility when it is warranted, while at the same time repelling projections.

Feels Superior

It is possible that both the inflated self and the poor me self exist at the same time in the same person. This person acts on both, but may not be fully aware of either. One state can assume prominence and be the source for much of that person's attitudes and behavior. The inflated self is seen in the attitudes of superiority and grandiosity and through the associated behaviors, such as boasting and devaluing others. It is much harder to describe the attitudes and the person's inner feelings, as these are internal, personal to that person, and can only be inferred by other people.

Your partner may feel superior and you only identify this attitude, after a considerable amount of time has passed. It's not always obvious and you probably tend to miss the signs. Because of your romantic involvement, it has taken time for your awareness to emerge. This superior attitude can be inferred from some of the following:

- Self-promotional statements that are frequent and intense.

- Devaluing and demeaning remarks about practically everyone else.

- A definite tendency to find faults and be picky.

- Demands of perfection from others, while ignoring or minimizing their own flaws or errors.

- Dismissive of input from others considered as inferior.

These are only some examples of what your partner may be feeling or doing that reflects their superior attitude. Items 7, 8, and 10 from the Manipulative DNP Scale are examples.

This is an attitude about which you can do nothing. It is a continuation of the infant's and child's perception of their self as all-powerful and all-knowing. There was not the expected growth and development, through which the person gradually recognized that there are other people and accepted the self as distinct and separate from others. Nor was there a recognition and acceptance that they would not be abandoned or destroyed for not being perfect. Your partner is not aware of any of these issues, and you cannot make her aware. Your strategies are to give up trying to make them change the attitude of feeling superior and to not let the attitude trigger your feelings of not being good enough or being fatally flawed.

Contemptuous of Others

Along with feeling superior can be an attitude of contempt for others. This contempt takes the form of disdain and scorn that others are not as worthy, good, able, or deserving, and should be ashamed of their inadequacies. Common phrases that describe contemptuousness are:

- looking down their noses,

- being stuck up,

- looking with scorn upon,
- turning up one's nose at,
- giving a cold shoulder to,
- turning one's back on,
- slamming the door in someone's face,
- teaching someone their distance or place,
- leaving someone out in the cold, or
- keeping someone at arms length.

There are numerous ways to convey contempt.

It's sad to think that anyone has to have this attitude and exhibit these behaviors in the attempt to shore up internal feelings of inadequacy, or to combat the feeling of being fatally flawed. However, these are what fuel the superior attitude and the actions that convey contempt. You must accept that these attitudes and actions are a reflection of the person's inner convictions and assumptions that are deep-seated and of long duration.

It can be frustrating and infuriating to be on the receiving end of these attitudes and behaviors. It is very hurtful when it is your partner conveying this to you or to those nearest and dearest to you. You may have protested, confronted your partner to try and make her understand the negative effect of her behavior on you and others, or done other things to try to get her to change. None of which was effective. The best strategies are for you to deal with your feelings, use your emotional insulation, and give up trying to change your partner.

Boasts and Brags

"I'm better than you are" is the message not so well hidden in boasting and bragging. This is also extended to encompass accomplishments and possessions of others connected to the bragging or boasting person where the feats of others are presented as being outcomes for the person who is boasting or bragging. For example, think of the father who boasts of his son's athletic accomplishments at every opportunity. It's as if the son is succeeding only because of the father.

Boasting and bragging, for this discussion, are described as continual announcements and constant inflation of events, actions, and possessions that are considered a part of the self. Thus, bragging and boasting are ways that people can announce to the world how great they are. It's much more than simple pride and pleasure for accomplishments, as the need to have others know about it and to arouse admiration or envy is very deep and intense. Having pride and taking pleasure in your accomplishments, your children's accomplishments, and those of other people who are connected to you is expected and supported. The difference is that those who brag and boast will seize every opportunity to do so, even to the extent that they will horn in on someone else's spotlight and use that opportunity to further brag and boast about themselves.

If this description fits your partner, then you probably have felt embarrassed at times to hear her brag or boast. If you have children and they are not given full credit for their accomplishments but are praised and bragged about because your partner is taking a great deal of the credit, you may also have felt frustrated and angry. In the latter case, it would be helpful for you to remember that destructive narcissists consider others as extensions of their self, and not as separate and distinct individuals. Thus, when your partner brags about her children, she is bragging about herself, and is convinced that she was not only instrumental in her children's accomplishments, but also caused it to happen.

Underlying the boasting and bragging is the need for reassurance that the person is approved of, admired, and indeed competent. It could be that this person did not receive this reassurance as an infant or during childhood, and continues to need and seek it. However, they do not recognize this need, can never receive enough reassurance, and are unaware that the need for reassurance is why they boast and brag. The reality may be that this too is a characteristic about which you can do nothing; it's up to that person.

Engages in Seductive Behavior

This is a behavior that is also characteristic of the Exhibitionist DNP. The person with a Manipulative DNP can have this characteristic, but will use it in a different way. This person uses it to:

- further their one-upmanship,
- put something over,
- reinforce their superiority,

- show others as unworthy or inferior, or

- take unfair advantage, as an opportunity to reinforce that they are correct in their contempt of others.

They seduce in a variety of ways, but every way allows them to prey on an unconscious need that the other person has. For example, if someone has a need for admiration, the Manipulative destructive narcissist will take every opportunity to be admiring of that person. It's really hard to see through their behavior when they are giving you what you want, even though you are not consciously aware that you want it.

Another way they are able to seduce is through violations of psychological boundaries when these boundaries are weak or spongy. The seduction is unconscious, as are the boundary violations. This topic is addressed in more detail in chapter 9. If you find that your partner is continually able to get you to do things you do not wish to do, then you will want to examine your boundary strength and begin to develop strong and resilient boundaries, so as to be able to resist being seduced.

Tries to Arouse Envy

Your Manipulative destructive narcissist partner may engage in behaviors and other acts that are intended to arouse envy from others. Your partner wants others to realize that she is unique and special, superior, more deserving and more worthy, and should be admired and envied. This is a craving that incorporates several destructive narcissistic characteristics, as described in chapters 1 and 2.

The attempts to arouse envy can take many forms.

- Boasting and bragging.

- Arrogance.

- Keeping the spotlight focused on them.

- Cheating, lying, or deception.

- Overspending or going into debt to buy things to be shown off.

- Nominating oneself for awards and other honors.

- Demanding more than one's fair share and making everyone know when it is received.

- Showing off.

- Doing things just to be noticed.

These are but a few of the most obvious examples of actions designed to arouse envy.

This need to be envied may also extend to you. You may not recognize that your partner wants your envy. You may think that your partner just overspends, spends foolishly, is trying to compensate for earlier deprivation or poverty, or is proud of what she has accomplished and enjoys having nice things. All these may be true, to some extent, but you are overlooking some signs that the need and craving is deep-rooted and long lasting. Signs of craving include:

- fishing for flattery and compliments,

- becoming upset when her accomplishments or possessions are not noted,

- appearing to be attracted only to people who are constantly admiring her,

- emphasizing her accomplishments or possessions at every opportunity, or

- never being satisfied with accomplishments or possessions.

You can use these as signs of the need and craving to be envied. In addition, if your partner has a Manipulative DNP, she may also engage in acts that have potential for ensuring that her accomplishments or possessions are such that they arouse envy. Examples of such acts include off-loading blame, cheating, making misleading statements, lying, and devaluing anyone thought to be in her way or who has the potential for being envied.

This too is an attitude with accompanying behaviors about which you can do nothing. Your partner does not recognize what she is doing, nor why she is doing it. Your discussions, confrontations, or challenges will fail, and by doing any of these you reinforce your partner's idea that you are also trying to destroy her and do not understand. The roots of this attitude are too long and deep for you to make any meaningful headway.

Your Collaborative Behaviors and Attitudes

You may be engaging in some behaviors or have some attitudes that encourage and support your Manipulative destructive narcissist partner, although it is without conscious intent. Indeed, your partner may well have been attracted to you because of this. The list in the following scale comprises only a few of such behaviors and attitudes that can exist, but can serve as a guide for your self-exploration and for possible changes you may wish to make.

Table 2: Manipulative DNP Scale

Directions: Rate yourself on each item using the scale.	
5—Always or almost always do or feel this 4—Frequently do or feel this 3—Sometimes do or feel this 2—Seldom do or feel this 1—Never or almost never do or feel this	
1. Fail to be assertive	
2. Fail to assert boundaries	
3. Become susceptible to emotional contagion (catching others' emotions)	
4. Are susceptible to flattery	
5. Have a strong need to be helpful to others	
6. Feel responsible when others are blaming you for their discomfort	
7. Can be made to feel ungrateful or wrong	
8. Are easily aroused to sympathy for others	
9. Feel that others will care for you as you care for them	
10. Trust others to have your best interests at heart	
Total _____	

Scoring

Add your ratings. A score of 40–50 indicates considerable collaborative behaviors; 30–39 indicates many behaviors; 20–29 indicate some behaviors; and less than 20 indicates few or none.

Fail to Be Assertive

When you fail to be assertive, or are passive, you invite others to control you. If you are aggressive, you run the risk of negatively impacting the relationship, or in the case of a Manipulative destructive narcissistic partner, of being perceived as a challenge to their manipulative skills. It can be a fine line between being passive and aggressive, when you are being assertive to preserve your integrity, rights and responsibilities, personal standards, and to ward off violations of your psychological boundaries.

If you are susceptible to catching other's emotions, you may fail to be assertive because you are acting on your partner's projections. This acceptance of the other person's projections is probably not limited to your partner, and also happens with other people. This tendency can contribute to your passivity.

Even if you tend to be aggressive in your responses, your Manipulative destructive narcissistic partner may be able to control you. Your partner learns to:

- push your buttons,

- get you emotionally intense, where you do not think clearly,

- con you into thinking that what you are doing or saying is over the top or out of line,

- point out that you are insensitive and hurtful, and

- use a host of other manipulative techniques.

You are fighting hard, but you are not succeeding.

To be more assertive, you can:

- build your emotional insulation, so that you can more easily repel others' projections;

- fortify your psychological boundaries, so that you reduce your identification with projections;

- reduce your emotional susceptibility to and moderate the triggering of your distressing feelings;

- begin to verbalize your rights and responsibilities without becoming hurt, upset, or angry; and

- say "no" and stick to it.

Your Boundaries

If you find that your partner can easily manipulate you to do what she wants you to do and not what you feel is in your best interests or what you want to do, then your boundaries are not being recognized, nor are they strong and resilient enough to withstand assault. These boundaries are the defining point of where you end and where others begin, and are recognition for you and the other person of separateness and distinctness as individuals. They are very important, as part of protection for the self, and are a crucial part of one's development of healthy adult narcissism.

One way to judge the strength of your boundaries is to reflect on the level and extent to which you become enmeshed or overwhelmed by other people's feelings. Do you easily take on the feelings other people have, such as becoming upset when they are upset? Do you sometimes feel that you are trying to remain detached from someone's emotional intensity, but find that you still become emotionally intense? If this happens to you, then you are becoming enmeshed or overwhelmed. If one or both of these are descriptive of what happens to you with your partner, you may find that she seems to be able to easily manipulate you.

It will not be easy for you to prevent becoming enmeshed or overwhelmed for two reasons. You will not be able to use many of the nonverbal strategies because of the intimacy of your relationship, and it takes time and considerable effort to build and fortify your psychological boundaries. Your partner will not be cooperative, as stronger and more resilient boundaries mean that you will not be as easily manipulated, and she will not be able to get from you whatever is wanted, needed, or desired. If you do pursue building stronger boundaries, be prepared for considerable resistance from your partner.

Susceptibility to Emotional Contagion

This item is closely associated with the previous one, in which your boundaries are not recognized. This leaves you open to emotional contagion, by which you catch other people's feelings, and your partner uses your susceptibility to her advantage.

This emotional susceptibility means that you are the receiver of others' emotions and that your boundaries and defenses are not sufficient to prevent your incorporation of and identification with them. In essence, you lose your sense of self, as being apart from the other person, and become open and receptive to whatever they are feeling. Once you incorporate these feelings, you are more likely to act on them. If the sender stays in touch with the receiver and the feelings, and you identify with the feelings, you can be manipulated by the sender. Either way, you are not fully in control of what you are doing or feeling, and are not making conscious decisions. You may even have a nagging sense of something that doesn't feel right to you, but you cannot identify what that something is.

If this description fits you, then you are probably in a relationship with a powerful sender, and you are the emotionally susceptible receiver. Your best strategy is to build your psychological boundaries, to the extent that you can screen out senders' projections, but can retain the ability to be appropriately empathic. This is not a simple or short-term process, and you have to be prepared to work very hard on your personal issues, faulty assumptions, and unfinished business, as these contain the basic causes for your emotional susceptibility. This work is best done with the help of a competent therapist. The suggestions and exercises in this book are some resources to get you started and can help guide some self-reflection.

Susceptible to Flattery

The Manipulative destructive narcissist can be very charming and seductive, and within their arsenal of techniques is the ability to sense your need and susceptibility to flattery. Flattery is insincere praise or other comments designed to have you think that you are admired, that the other person thinks you are unique and special, and that you are of value to the person making these comments. You may indeed be all of these, but the intent of the flatterer is to have you become more open to their manipulation.

The Manipulative destructive narcissist uses flattery to control others, as a way to gain power over the other person, to support her personal feelings of superiority, and to have evidence that others are gullible and inferior as validation of her inflated or grandiose self. The amount of sincerity in her comments is scant or nonexistent. She can remain unaware of her real reasons for flattering you, while she gains much pleasure from having you positively respond, as she is putting one over on you.

Your susceptibility to flattery has many of the same roots as the tendency to be emotionally susceptible. That is, this need for admiration is buried in your unresolved family-of-origin issues, unfinished business, or faulty assumptions. These can be resolved with a commitment to working on them with time, effort, and responsible guidance from a competent therapist. Some understanding of these can be gained from self-reflection and an exploration of personal assumptions that may not be logical or rational. In the short term, you could try some self-talk when your partner or others make flattering comments to and about you. Instead of gulping them down unexamined, try asking yourself the following important questions: Why is this comment making me feel good, admired, pleased, etc.? What is the hidden agenda? Can I feel good about myself, even if I don't believe they are sincere? What's the worst thing that can happen if the comment is not true? What does this person want from me?

Need to be Helpful

Your caring and concern for others' welfare may be an important part of who you are, and you value that part of your self. You may have been reinforced for your helpfulness and thoughtfulness, and now you don't know or want to be any other way. It makes you feel good to be of help, and you reach out every chance you get. Others may even have come to depend on you for help are very appreciative of your help, and you like how this makes you feel.

The other side of your caring and concern may not be personally rewarding. You may find your need to be helpful is exploited by others to your disadvantage. You may find it difficult to say "no" or to refuse requests. You may feel you are being exploited, and it is at these times when you may wish that you did not have this strong need.

Associated with this strong need can be the feelings of guilt and shame that are aroused when you try to take care of yourself or when you refuse to be exploited. These feelings, along with your strong need to be helpful, give your Manipulative destructive narcissistic partner ample opportunities and room to exploit you for her needs. You will do almost anything to prevent these feelings from emerging, and your partner senses this. What you can work to change, in the short term, is having these feelings triggered. If you are not fighting feelings of guilt or shame, you have more energy to stay objective and rational. It's harder to manipulate someone who is thinking than it is to manipulate a person who is focused on feelings. One thing you can do is to make a habit of employing your emotional insulation, especially when you begin to feel that you need to, should, or ought to be helpful. Once your emotional insulation is in place, you can use some thought-stopping techniques, such as asking yourself, "Why do I think I need to take care of this person?" or "Can this person take care of herself?" In other words, go to your head, instead of staying focused on your heart. Questions like these will allow you to keep the wonderful part of caring and being helpful, and will stop you from having to inappropriately act on your need. If you want to change the intensity of this need, you will need to employ the long-term strategies described in the previous two items.

Feeling Responsible

When others are uncomfortable and seem to look to you for relief, do you feel responsible for not preventing the discomfort, or feel that you should do something to provide relief? If you do, then you probably have a strong sense of responsibility for others' well-being and welfare. That is, you feel that you are supposed to make sure that they do not suffer any discomfort. If this is a characteristic way of feeling and behaving for you, then you may be suffering the effects of having been a parentified child, where you were made to feel and be responsible for the emotional well-being of one or more of your parents. This situation is described in chapter 1. You are continuing to do for others what your parents expected of you, and your partner may be taking full advantage of your unconscious faulty assumption that you are responsible for others' comfort or discomfort. It's worse when others blame you, for then you have both external and internal blame to contend with, and this can be very distressing.

There are occasions when some or all of the responsibility is yours, and you can recognize these without much difficulty. However, what is not so easy for you to recognize is when you bear some, little, or no responsibility for other's discomfort. You rush to assume responsibility, apologize for not being better at preventing or eliminating the discomfort, and beat up on yourself in other ways. Your partner is especially good at allowing you to assume blame and responsibility.

It will not be easy for you to moderate or eliminate this feeling, as you may never have known any other way of feeling and behaving. However, it would be helpful for you to accept that you do not always bear responsibility for others' well-being, welfare, or discomfort, especially if the other person is a fully functioning adult. You do, of course, have some responsibility for the welfare and well-being of children and others who are dependent on you and cannot take care of themselves. But this responsibility lessens as children grow older and become more independent. You need to be careful that you are not stifling or delaying their growth and development toward independence and autonomy by not allowing them to assume responsibility for self-care.

Working on knowing when to take responsibility and when not to assume blame for others' discomfort will be difficult. You may need to explore the basis for this belief with a competent therapist in order to effect long-lasting changes. Short-term strategies can include using your emotional insulation to keep from having your guilt and shame aroused, and trying to step back and reflect when someone charges you with being responsible for their discomfort. Just taking a few seconds to think through the charges can allow you to become more aware that you are not to blame and can keep you from rushing to make it all better.

Feeling Ungrateful or Wrong

These feelings are versions of guilt and shame. They carry the messages that you are not quite good enough, that you do not measure up to expectations, that you ought to or should be different or better in some way, and that you need to atone or change. These are feelings that do not help self-esteem, self-confidence, or self-concepts. When you have these feelings, you may also be inclined to act on them and to try to get the person who is pointing out how ungrateful or wrong you are to change this perception.

This attitude is one that can allow your Manipulative destructive narcissistic partner to take advantage of you. Just because someone accuses you of being ungrateful or wrong does not mean that person is accurate. Nor are you under any compulsion to be grateful. No one is correct all of the time, and it is not shameful to be wrong.

You Are Sympathetic

Having sympathy for other people can indicate your caring and your ability to understand that they are enduring distress and discomfort. For example, sympathizing with someone who failed to get a promotion, or when someone loses a loved one, can be comforting to the other person, as the sympathy lets them know that you regret what they are experiencing. Sympathy can convey sorrow, regret, pity, and other ways of understanding.

The usual intent of sympathy is to give the other person a connection to someone that has some appreciation for what they may be feeling. Sympathy is detached, unlike empathy, where you enter the world of the other person and feel what that person is feeling. Sympathy is essentially your feeling, and what you think or project that the other person may be feeling. You are not in their world, nor are you feeling what they are feeling.

This last point is important for you to know and accept, as it is another way by which you can be manipulated by your partner with a DNP, and by others at times. That is, you think the other person is feeling a particular way, or you assume that they ought to be feeling a particular way, and because you are trying to make them feel better or to show your caring and concern, you are more open to being manipulated to do what that person wants you to do. Either way, the result is that you do things that you do not want to do or that are not in your best interest when you are sympathetic.

Your emotional susceptibility also plays a role, as you can catch the distress and become sympathetic. It is possible to be sympathetic without catching the other person's feeling, but if your sympathy is easily aroused, you may also be emotionally susceptible. This is particularly important for you to know about yourself if your partner has a DNP, because you are more likely to catch and act on your partner's distress and to be open to their manipulation.

There are several strategies that can help. Use your emotional insulation, think instead of feeling, recognize your limitations, and accept that others have responsibility for their own feelings. When you use your emotional insulation, you can prevent yourself from catching others' feelings and from having your uncomfortable feelings aroused. This can allow you to remain more detached and thoughtful, instead of catching and acting on someone's feelings, or of having your feelings intensified. You will be much less open to manipulation by other persons.

When you are detached, you can think instead of becoming mired in feelings. Thinking can help you reduce or eliminate attempts to manipulate you via your sympathy. Thinking can allow you to be more aware of what you want and need, and to dismantle faulty assumptions such as, "I should take care of _____ and get them to stop having those distressing feelings." You cannot cause someone to feel a particular way, and you need to recognize and accept your limitations in this respect. You are not responsible for others' feelings, and the guilty or shameful feelings you can have for not helping someone to feel better are not your responsibility. You did not fail, because you never had that power or control. If something you do or say does help the other person feel better, it is because they decided to let it do so.

Caring for Others

You may have the faulty assumption that if you care for others, then they will care for you. You may even be holding on to this faulty assumption in spite of evidence and experience throughout your life that point out its fallacy. Nevertheless, you continue to hold on to it, act on it, and allow yourself to be manipulated by it. No matter what disappointments you have encountered, when you cared and the other person did not, you've clung to the hope that the next relationship will be different.

Your faulty assumption, hope, and yearning are helpful to your Manipulative destructive narcissistic partner in controlling you. Your partner exploits your caring and concern for her, fails to reciprocate in kind, and is quick to point out when she feels you have been insensitive or not as caring as she wants you to be.

This faulty assumption springs from some of your early experiences, your fear of being abandoned, and the fear that you are not able to care for yourself. You have incorporated a message that you are incapable, inadequate, and must be dependent in order to survive. Deep-seated issues such as these cannot be adequately addressed in this book. The best that can be done is to make you aware of the possible presence of the issues, and how they may be helping your partner to manipulate you.

What can you do in the short-term? It could be helpful to give up the fantasy that if you care for someone, they will then care for you. It's nice when that happens, but letting go of the fantasy and expectation can give you a more realistic perspective. You can ask yourself if you fear that you won't be liked or cared for when you think you may be manipulated. If the answer is "yes," you can make self-affirming statements that you can care for yourself and that you will live if someone else does not look out for you. A little detachment and rational thought can do wonders.

Trusting Others

If trusting others to have your best interests at heart is one of your characteristics, you are leaving yourself open to disappointment, hurt, manipulation, and other dangers. Some people in your life may have your best interests at heart, but even those who say that they do can be using you to meet their needs. This can be especially true for your destructive narcissistic partner, who is simply self-absorbed and can only consider what is in her best interest. There may be times when both your interests and those of your partner coincide, but this is only happenstance.

Your trusting of others, especially in the face of evidence to the contrary, is a fantasy and yearning for someone to care for and love you. It could be associated with your not receiving the empathy, unconditional positive regard, and love that you wanted and needed early in life, and on an unconscious level, you continuously look to others to provide it.

You are going to have to change your expectations and attitude to something more realistic. Your partner and others are not going to change and begin to have your best interests at heart. You will be very lucky to have someone in your life who does and you should cherish that person. You may need to adopt a protective attitude of looking out for your own best interests and giving up the fantasy.

Whenever you find yourself being cajoled into doing something you don't want to do by your partner, and you are very aware that you don't want to do it, but rationalize that your partner would not ask you to do anything that wasn't in your best interests, stop at that point. Stop and remind yourself that you have to look out for your best interests, because your partner is looking out for her interests, and the two may be incompatible. You do not have to do something that you do not want to do. You are in charge of that decision, and you need to stop trusting that someone else has your best interests at heart.

Chapter 8

The Exhibitionist Destructive Narcissistic Pattern

Lights! Camera! Action! This could be the motto of the person with an Exhibitionist DNP. Grand actions that are designed to garner attention, admiration, and envy are an integral part of this person, and everything he does, says, feels, and believes. It's more than being extroverted. This person is:

- impulsive,
- reckless,
- seductive,
- controlling,
- intense, but remote,
- haughty,
- arrogant and cocky, and
- always "on stage."

Table 1: Exhibitionist DNP Scale

Directions: If much of this fits your partner, rate them on the scale that follows.	
5—Always or almost always 4—Frequently 3—Sometimes 2—Seldom 1—Never or almost never	
1. Makes grand entrances or exits	
2. Does and says things to get attention	
3. Engages in reckless behavior	
4. Focuses on his external body appearance excessively	
5. Is cold and haughty	
6. Exaggerates and inflates his accomplishments or acquisitions	
7. Seeks admiration for sexual prowess	
8. Speaks loudly and interrupts others	
9. Is very seductive, but also rejecting	
10. Plays to the audience	
Total _____	

Scoring

Add the ratings. A score of 40–50 indicates considerable exhibitionist characteristics; 30–39 indicates many of these characteristics; 20–29 indicates some characteristics; and below 20 indicates that there are a few or none of these characteristics.

Grand Entrances and Exits

These are attention-getting strategies. People who make grand entrances and exits want to make sure that they are noticed. There may also be some elements of admiration seeking and wanting to be envied. It's almost as though if they were unobtrusive, then they would disappear. It is only through the attention of other people that this person achieves validation that he or she does indeed exist.

These grand entrances and exits may even be planned to maximize their impact. By staging such things, the person can be reasonably assured that each and every eye will be focused on them.

Examples of grand entrances include the following:

- Arriving late and making a lot of noise.

- Announcing to everyone the intent to leave.

- Wearing clothes that are designed to get attention (for example, transparent or very tight garments).

- Interrupting the event and loudly apologizing.

- Breezing in and saying, "Sorry, I'm late."

- Deliberately waiting for the event or meeting to begin before entering.

There are numerous ways to make grand entrances and exits, and this person can make use of all of them. They become upset when these do not work, and strive harder to get the needed attention.

Seeks Attention

Masked by the grandness and inflated self-perception is an impoverished ego state that is still trying to get the attention that was denied as an infant or child. They did not get their attention needs met, and while there may be a variety of legitimate reasons why the parent or caretaker did not sufficiently meet these needs, the deficit is still having a major impact at a deep and unconscious level. This does not necessarily mean that the infant or child was neglected, but what did happen was that he did not receive the attention that he needed. Some examples of possible reasons include: parental illness, maternal depression, numerous siblings close in age that also needed attention, absence of one or more parents for an extended period of time, and parental alcohol or substance abuse. The adult who had these early circumstances is continually trying to get this need for attention taken care of, but can never get enough.

If this fits your partner, you are in a position where you are expected to give continual attention, such as that needed for an infant or child, although your partner is an adult. You cannot talk him out of this need, nor can you give him enough attention to fill the need. He will continue to seek attention from everyone in his world, and will become angry when he does not receive it.

Does your partner do or say things to get attention? Things that are offensive, sarcastic, off-the-wall but not funny, hurtful, or demeaning? Have you been embarrassed, humiliated, or shamed by acts and remarks that were directed to you or at others? Have you tried to get your partner to stop doing or saying these things by telling him about the negative impact of the acts or words on you and others, only to have your partner ignore or dismiss your efforts? Did you recognize that your partner was doing or saying these things to get attention? The Exhibitionist destructive narcissist doesn't just inflate his accomplishments or brag and boast to get attention. This person also has to show superiority by highlighting others' inadequacies, inferiority, unworthiness, flaws, and other faults. He thinks that he is so much better than others, and that others need to have this difference emphasized in a public forum, so that everyone can be aware of just how much these people are failing to be good enough.

One of the worst responses to this behavior is to become hurt. When you show that these acts or remarks are wounding to you, the Exhibitionist destructive narcissist seizes this opportunity to characterize you as denying the truth, unable to face the facts, or as overreacting. The battleground shifts, and while you continue to try to deal with the original remarks, your partner is fighting on another front and you don't even know it. It sounds harsh to say, and it is harsh, but your partner is indifferent to your hurt feelings. Your partner is convinced that he has the right to do or say whatever he wants to, and that others should accept the "rightness" of the act or remarks.

Other responses that are not constructive or productive are to go on the offensive and attack, or to become defensive. You will just make bad matters worse. It will be difficult for you to not do any of what was discussed, but you will be less frustrated, hurt, angry, embarrassed, or humiliated if you:

- can use your emotional insulation,
- do not take responsibility for your partner's acts or remarks,
- recognize that your partner is seeking attention,
- limit your responses to being neutral or noncommittal,
- change the subject,
- say something like, "Really?" and then move on, or
- try to give your partner attention in more constructive ways.

Reckless Behavior

"A walk on the wild side" could be said to characterize this behavior. This person takes unreasonable chances, just for the thrill, which provides opportunities for bragging and boasting. You may have even been attracted to your partner in part because of their reckless behavior. Your partner did exciting things, took chances, was very dashing, and you longed to be like that, or at least be close to someone who did those things.

What you probably didn't realize was that this behavior was constant, continual, and very risky. Reckless behavior is not limited to physical events, such as driving well over the speed limit. There are other behaviors, and these people will engage in more than one kind. Examples include:

- gambling beyond one's means,
- lying to authorities,
- embezzling and other white collar criminal acts,
- engaging in risky sexual encounters,
- substance use and abuse,
- walking or going to unsafe places,
- goading a very dangerous person,
- being argumentative or combative in an unsafe place, or
- associating with dangerous people.

These and other reckless behaviors put lives and welfare at risk just to experience thrills and excitement.

There is also an element of the child's and adolescent's attitude of invincibility for these people. They really don't believe that anything negative will happen as a result of their reckless behavior, because of their superiority, and because it has not happened yet. You can see the grandiosity, omnipotence, superior attitude, wanting attention, needs for admiration, and the need to be envied throughout their behaviors and attitudes.

You will not be able to moderate, change, or eliminate their reckless behavior. You may need to take steps to protect yourself and your family from the consequences of these behaviors, such as excessive compulsive gambling. That will be about the best you can do.

Excessive Body Focus

The Exhibitionist destructive narcissist may give an inordinate amount of time, attention, and money to the preservation of his body's external appearance. This person is not only admiring of his appearance, he is also contemptuous of those who are not as attractive, well dressed, fit, or young looking. This person seeks bodily perfection as a means to gain admiration, attention, and envy.

What is meant here is more than just caring about your external appearance; it is an excessive focus. These are the people who, for example:

- can spend a great deal of time looking in mirrors,

- are fanatic about working out,

- make disparaging comments about others' physical appearance,

- expect compliments about their appearance,

- dress to attract remarks and to show off their bodies,

- can seek perfection through cosmetic surgery, not just to feel or look better, or

- get upset at the least sign of physical aging, and cannot get over it.

Nothing seems as important to these people as their physical appearance.

The sad thing is that they can never get enough attention, admiration, and envy. They do not build their relationships, creativity, altruism, and so forth. They stay stuck in this self-absorption. They refuse to grow and develop in other ways. They can deny their mortality to the extent that they fail to heed warning signs of medical conditions or disease, and can refuse to make needed life changes, for example, moving to a less stressful job after having two heart attacks. You cannot do or say anything that will effect a positive change or a more mature perspective.

Cold and Haughty

Cold and haughty are words that describe someone who is aloof, detached, and empty at the core of self. These are the people who have a need to be superior, for fear that, in fact, they are not superior. They can have a superficial charm that attracts others and are able to fake caring and concern, but are not able to establish meaningful and satisfying relationships. They never really connect to anyone, but are able to fool many people.

This coldness can be seen in their indifference to the negative impact of their behavior and attitudes on others, their insensitive and demeaning comments to and about others, their lack of empathy, their need to exploit others for personal gain, and other similar behavior and attitudes. The lack of warmth and caring for others is closely tied to the emptiness within the person. A void that is an integral part of the person is of long standing. Neither you nor anyone else can begin to fill this void, but this person continually seeks the "magic" person who can fill the emptiness, help them connect to others in meaningful ways, and reduce those feelings of isolation and alienation. You do not fail to meet their need; it is a need that no one, except the person themselves, can fulfill.

The haughty behavior is the external manifestation of the coldness within. Haughtiness is seen in descriptors such as the following:

- looking down their nose,
- nose stuck up in the air,
- an air of contempt,
- indifference to the existence of others,
- arrogance, and
- cutting, biting, and sarcastic comments to and about others.

The haughty person holds himself above and superior to others, and works hard at making sure that everyone is conscious of his superiority.

You may have been attracted to this person because you viewed the haughtiness as confidence. It was only after considerable experience that you were able to see the coldness and attitude of superiority behind the charm. This person was attentive and flattering, and you responded favorably. You remained unaware that he did not really connect with you in a meaningful way, became disappointed that you were not able to fill his inner void, and he began to discount you as worthy of his attention. Notice that in all this, you are perceived as insufficient and failing. Your partner can never entertain any possibility that he is insufficient or has failed in any way, or has expectations that are impossible to fulfill. Your partner remains unaware of the void within, and nothing you do or say can make them aware. You failed, because there was no way to succeed. You do not have the power to change any of this, to provide a meaningful and satisfying relationship for them, or to begin to fill their internal void.

Exaggerates and Inflates Self

Exhibitionist destructive narcissists will often exaggerate and inflate those aspects of self that they want admired. These can be personal attributes, possessions, acts, or just about anything. Everything about them is bigger, grander, better, and more important than what others have, do, or are. Ordinary events and situations take on a dramatic quality when this person is involved. There is no such thing as quiet, unobtrusiveness, or subtlety for anything that they are involved with or attached to.

This tendency to exaggerate and inflate also extends to their responses to you and others, especially when assigning blame, criticism, or fault. They use terms like, "you always" and "you never," even when it is apparent that these are not accurate. For example, one time you forget to pick up the clothes from the cleaner, and your partner says, "You always forget to pick up the clothes." Your response may be to protest that "always" is not accurate, but your partner does not buy that, and you are left with some uncomfortable feelings, such as frustration and anger. It would be less troubling to you to realize that:

- your partner will exaggerate any perceived fault of yours,

- because your partner says something does not mean it is so, and

- you do not have to allow your uncomfortable feelings to be triggered.

You can ignore the superlatives and keep the focus on the less threatening content. For example, in the previously described situation, you could respond with, "Always is a bit of an exaggeration. I did forget today. I'll try to make sure it doesn't happen again." A response like this can defuse the situation and negative feelings.

One final note about the Exhibitionist destructive narcissist's exaggeration and inflation: this person does this only for his benefit. Even when he appears to be doing this for someone else, there is a part that focuses on him and how wonderful he must be, or that he contributed in some way to the other person's accomplishments. It is almost as if he were saying that he *caused* the other person's success.

Sexual Prowess

Many who have an Exhibitionist DNP openly solicit admiration for their sexual prowess. They want others to admire and envy them for being sexually attractive or more successful and better at sexual games. They seek to be the fantasized lover with many conquests and a string of broken hearts. This provides them with much satisfaction and validation that they are superior, worthy, admired, and envied. These people do not know of any other way to connect to others except through sexual means.

If this description fits your partner, you may find that your partner is constantly flirting, cruising, trolling, engaging in affairs, and not exactly keeping this a secret. His efforts at being secretive wouldn't fool a two-year-old child. You may also find that your partner is depreciative and dismissive of you as a sexual partner and blames you for his wanderings. Where once you were satisfying, you now fail to meet your partner's expectations. No matter how hard you try, you never seem to be good enough, and this is his excuse for getting sexually involved with other people.

No one can ever be good enough for these people, because what they are looking for is what they did not get early in life. They flit from person to person and are always disappointed. There are times when they think they have found the ideal person who meets this need, but this person too will disappoint after a while, and so they move on. The need for visibility of their sexual exploits is also a part of this deep-seated longing for meaningful and satisfying connections with others. They think that if others can see how wonderful they are, this will validate their feelings of being unique, special, and superior.

You will not be able to meet these deep-seated and long lasting needs, nor will anyone else be able to meet them. You cannot change your partner, and you have to make a personal decision about what you are willing to tolerate.

Is Loud and Interrupts

Whispering, a soft voice, or even a regular voice is not sufficient or satisfying for this person. He is loud most of the time and may tend to talk constantly. It's almost as if he cannot think unless he is also verbalizing, and he thinks out loud most of the time. This is the person who makes sure that he is heard at every turn and about almost everything.

This person may also feel entitled to interrupt almost everyone. That is, he will interrupt those he feels are of lower status. You may find that your partner frequently interrupts you. Whatever your partner wants, needs, or desires is much more important than what you have to say. Your partner may even talk while you are talking, in an effort to gain the spotlight.

Attention is one goal of these behaviors and asserting superiority is another goal. Never forget that these people do not want to share the attention, and they consider themselves to be superior to you and everyone else. Their charm can mask this basic assumption, but it is still there. Any attention you or others may be receiving will soon be deflected to them.

Unless you are willing to become aggressive, engage in shouting contests, or refuse to yield the spotlight, you are limited in what effective strategies you have available. These three are *not recommended,* as you will be perceived very negatively by others involved at the time. They will not understand why you are speaking so loudly, attacking your partner, or any other similar behaviors. You will lose on all counts, and you don't want to do that. You can try ignoring these behaviors and proceed as if they did not exist. What can be troubling, however, are the uncomfortable feelings that may be aroused. If you become angry, hurt, irritated, frustrated, embarrassed, or the like, you can thoughtfully step back and tell yourself that you are not responsible for your partner's behavior, that he craves the attention, and that you are adult enough not to get into a contest with him. It can also be effective to calmly finish what you were saying before you were interrupted. Don't belabor the point that you were interrupted, just finish what you intended to say.

Seductive but Rejecting

Charming, seductive, attractive, and appealing can all be used to describe Exhibitionist destructive narcissists. Their flamboyance, grandness, the air of danger about them, the totality of their attention to those they are interested in at the moment combine to draw others to them. Others are seduced into opening up and giving of their self at times, without fully realizing what is happening. This is seduction in the sense that the Exhibitionist destructive narcissist has no emotional investment in the other person, does not value them as a worthwhile, unique person, is indifferent to this person's needs, and has only a self-focus as a central concern.

However, the Exhibitionist destructive narcissist is very successful at seduction and never lacks for a responsive conquest. There is always someone who buys into the illusion that they are the most interesting and attractive person that the Exhibitionist destructive narcissist has ever encountered.

A difficulty with the seduction is that the Exhibitionist is, at the same time, rejecting of you, although this part is not perceived as such. Your partner can use the ploy of complimenting you for not being like someone else or for not having a characteristic like other people. For example, your partner may say such things as, "I really like that you don't do . . ." or "It irritates me when people do. . . , and I am glad you are not like that." You can respond by trying to tune in to what your partner dislikes to make sure you are different, just to keep his interest and attention. What you are not hearing and may not be aware of is that your partner will start to reject you at some point. Not for the same reasons that he stated about others; he will find other things about you that are unsatisfying, faulty, and inferior. His interest and attention will be given to someone else who does not have the same characteristic for which you are rejected, just as you captured his interest from someone else. No one can ever live up to the Exhibitionist destructive narcissist's expectations. Others constantly disappoint him, and he continues to search for the fantasized ideal. This search never ends and no one is ever good enough.

Plays to the Audience

The Exhibitionist destructive narcissist can be very adept at figuring out what will appeal to others, and will do whatever it takes to win their attention, admiration, and approval. It's like a game to this person, where they show superiority by being able to give others what they want, without their knowing what that something is or the Exhibitionist having to be told what is wanted. It can be uncanny the way that they accomplish this, but they do work hard at it.

It can be important for you to stay aware that whatever your Exhibitionist destructive narcissistic partner is doing or saying, he is playing to an audience. This means that your partner:

- is out to get what he wants by fair means or foul,
- seldom, if ever, is genuine and authentic,
- is very competitive in almost everything,
- seeks to manipulate and control,
- does not care about, or is indifferent to, others' needs,
- is not satisfied with less than total and unqualified attention and admiration,
- is always intent on self-needs or self-focus,
- is very demanding that you trust them, but does not trust you, or
- is almost always "on stage."

Your task is to understand how your partner perceives you as the audience and is performing or playing to you. Until you get to this point, you are open to hurt, humiliation, manipulation, and an erosion of your self-confidence and self-esteem.

Your Collaborative Behavior and Attitudes

You may have some personal characteristics that unwittingly encourage your Exhibitionist destructive narcissistic partner. From the beginning of the relationship, you saw the grandness, the inflated self-perception, and the need for attention and admiration, as they are not exactly subtle, shy, or retiring. You did not see, or did allow yourself to be aware of, the more negative aspects of your partner's behaviors and attitudes, as you were dazzled and swept away.

It could be helpful for you to understand yourself a little better and to become aware of what personal behaviors and attitudes of yours are playing into your partner's hands and allowing him to manipulate and control you. Even if you are trying to resist being manipulated and controlled, you can find that this continues to happen and you don't know why. Let's explore some possible behaviors and attitudes that could be contributing.

Table 2: Exhibitionist DNP Collaborative Behaviors and Attitudes Scale

Directions: Rate yourself on the following items using the following scale.	
5—Always or very much like you 4—Frequently like you 3—Sometimes like you 2—Seldom or a little like you 1—Never or almost never like you	
1. Willing to assume a subordinate role	
2. Drawn to and admire reckless behavior	
3. Bask in the glow of reflected admiration	
4. Sacrifice so your partner can buy clothes and other items to enhance his image	
5. Accept his frequent excuses for forgetting birthdays and other important occasions	
6. Devalue and blame others who are critical of your partner	

7. Feel really displeased when your partner does not receive attention or admiration from others	
8. Assume the major responsibility for the care of the family or marriage	
9. Make excuses for his insensitive behavior and attitudes	
10. Are conscious of status	
Total _____	

Scoring

Add your ratings. A score of 40–50 indicates that you have a considerable number of collaborative behaviors and attitudes; 30–39 indicates many such behaviors and attitudes; 20–29 indicates some of these; and below 20 indicates few or none of the behaviors and attitudes.

The Subordinate Role

There is room for only one star in the Exhibitionist destructive narcissist's world, and he is it. Don't make the mistake of thinking that your partner will share the spotlight at some point, as he will not ever do this. If, for some reason, you are getting attention and admiration, your partner will snatch it away, disparage you, or make sure you cannot enjoy it. All attention and admiration should be his, in his way of thinking.

Thus, you are expected to assume a subordinate role at all times and give your partner deference for being so superior and grand. If you are willing to do this, then your partner can continue to garner the available spotlight with the accompanying attention, and you may retain his approval. The catch here is that, even if you do stay in a subordinate role, his approval of you can diminish, because, on an unconscious level, he knows that the impoverished self is there and is not deserving of the admiration and attention. You are admiring something that your partner feels is not good enough, and your partner can begin to despise you for that, or he can sense when you lessen your attention and admiration and he can become very angry, vengeful, and rejecting.

Another possibility is that you will fail to continue to grow and develop your self, talent, and abilities when you remain always in a subordinate role. Your focus and efforts are on your partner, instead of being shared. There can be times when the focus should be on your partner, but you also merit some focus.

Admire Reckless Behavior

You may have been drawn to your partner because he seemed so dashing, was able to take chances and succeed, was extraordinary, and had other larger-than-life characteristics and behaviors. Your partner stood out from the crowd and was anything but mundane, and you were intrigued and captured by his exploits, attitude, and confidence to take chances.

You may have known of his reckless behavior, as he would boast and brag about his success in taking chances, going to the edge, and other ways of being reckless. You may even have been appalled or scared as you heard about his exploits, but you were also excited and thrilled. He did things or acted as you wished you could act or be, and you were attracted.

On some level, you know that a very real outcome for this behavior is failure, and consequences could be devastating and dire. You may fear the outcome and the consequences, and this fear keeps you from engaging in reckless behavior. You also are aware that just because the outcome and the consequences of this behavior are positive in some instances, this does not mean they will continue to be positive. You knew all this, but still you were captivated by your partner's reckless behavior and did not realize that this behavior would extend to other parts of his life.

You will benefit from examining your fascination with this kind of behavior, why and how you admire it, even though openly you may decry it, and exploring how you can become excited and thrilled in other ways. You will not change your partner, but you can understand and protect yourself better with this self-knowledge.

Reflected Glory

Associated with the previous item can be a tendency for you to bask in the reflection of admiration that your partner receives. Do you get a feeling of being superior to those who don't have a partner who receives admiration? Do you like, or are you thrilled by others thinking you are special because of your partner and his exploits? Do you get special attention because of who your partner is or for what your partner does? Does any of this reflected admiration make you feel closer to your partner?

If any of this resonates with you, then you are getting a charge out of your partner's reflected glory. It is called reflected because you do not receive it for who you are or for what you do, but only because you are identified as connected to your partner. You may even be dedicated to helping your partner get even more admiration, instead of working to develop your own abilities and talents.

You can begin to take a serious look at yourself and note how you have not given yourself the time, attention, and effort needed to develop your abilities and talents. This does not mean that you withdraw your support for your partner and only concentrate on yourself. It means you turn to getting your charge or thrill from what you are able to do and be, and not the reflection of your partner's accomplishments.

Personal Sacrificing

Do you sacrifice your personal or family needs so that your partner can buy things just to stay in fashion, be one step ahead of the neighbors, or show off? Is your partner the first one to get use of the family resources for whatever they feel is needed, and are you agreeable to that? Do you make numerous personal sacrifices just so your partner can shine or be admired? If you see yourself in any of these, you are subordinating and abasing your own, and possibly your family's, needs. You and your family are getting the message that your partner is of more value.

There are times when your partner's needs are of priority, and this is to be expected and respected. However, sacrifice is not supposed to be one-way, where your personal needs are always taking a back seat to those of your partner. You are willingly cooperating with your partner's desires to get attention, be admired, and be envied. You are not paying enough attention to taking care of yourself, and may be putting your children in a position where they feel less important, worthy, and valued.

Since personal sacrificing is not an all-or-nothing situation, you can become more judicious in selecting when it is important to make these sacrifices. My personal bias is that children always come first. Their needs are of most importance and must be of first priority. If these can be met, then whatever you decide is of priority or importance at that particular time is acceptable. That is, you can judge whether your partner's needs are more important or if yours are. There is no cut or dried way to make a decision, as each situation and relationship is different. The only guideline is that there should be some times and situations in which you do not have to make personal sacrifices.

Accept Excuses

You may have experienced your partner's frequent forgetting of your birthday, anniversary, and other personally important events. There always seems to be some reason for the forgetfulness, and he makes pledges to do better next time, but it happens over and over again. You are understanding; you forgive the lapses and try to behave as if it were not important to you. After all, you are an adult, and these special days are not as meaningful as they once were, or so you rationalize. You may even deny to yourself that you are disappointed.

The most important point is that your partner is insensitive, indifferent, and uncaring, not that he forgot. Forgetting can happen to everyone, and there are occasions when life circumstances intervene to become more urgent and important. These times, of course, call for your understanding. Let's hope they are few and far in-between. What is meant here is that there is almost always some excuse, usually a lame one, for forgetting, and that you tend to accept it.

Why would you continue to let yourself be discounted, pushed aside, forgotten, and devalued in this way? Do you not consider yourself to be important enough and of enough value to have these times remembered by your partner? After all, you probably make an effort to recognize their birthday, anniversary, and other personally important events, and you should be able to expect reciprocity. You may want to do some self-exploration about your willingness to accept this kind of behavior. Your partner is not about to change, and there is little you can do to address their forgetting of your personally important remembrances. Even noting dates on calendars or leaving notes are unlikely to produce the desired result. You are not on their radar screen, and there is only room for one person in their self focus.

Devalues and Blames

Are you so enmeshed with your partner that you devalue and blame anyone who criticizes them? Does this criticism hurt you? Do you feel that it is others who are critical and unfair, jealous, and failing to do their part or to recognize the true worth of your partner? Does it feel like you are also being attacked? If these attitudes and feelings are descriptive of you, these may reflect considerable enmeshment with your partner, through which you are seeking fusion with him. You are taking on your partner's attitude and feelings and making them yours. This is one way you can lose your sense of self, fail to maintain the sense of difference between your partner and you, and limit your psychological growth and development.

You may think you are empathizing with your partner, but when you blame and devalue others for criticizing him, you are taking on your partner's impoverished self and making that a part of you. Just because someone is critical does not mean the person is correct or wrong. Whatever they say, it is their opinion, and they have a right to it, whatever it may be. You do not have to agree, accept, reject, or do anything with it. When you attack the critical person by devaluing or blaming them, you are not respecting that person's right to their opinion or their boundaries. What is most likely to be happening is that you are encouraging and supporting your partner's grandiosity, sense of superiority, and their inflated self by attacking or deriding others who criticize your partner.

Your task is to become more psychologically separated and individuated. That is, you need to understand at a deep level that you are a distinct and separate person and to develop your self identity. This will take some self-exploration and self-reflection, and can be facilitated by working with a competent therapist.

Feel Displeased

If you become irritated, angry, or upset when your partner does not receive the attention and admiration that he wants and you feel is deserved, you are again exhibiting some signs of enmeshment. You are assuming their attitudes and feelings, and not maintaining an appropriate psychological boundary. This is especially true if it happens often.

Partners who are close can become disappointed when their partner's efforts or accomplishments are not recognized, and understand what the partner may be feeling. However, they do not take on the partner's feelings and can remain more rational and objective. Partners who become enmeshed can be constantly upset because the Exhibitionist destructive narcissists can never get enough or sufficient attention and admiration. Thus, both of you remain upset and can go to extremes to get more and more attention and admiration.

The next time you begin to be displeased when your partner is not receiving sufficient attention and admiration, mentally step back and ask yourself:

- Why is this important to me?

- What do I hope to accomplish?

- What is the worst thing that could happen?

- Why do I feel this is about me?

The answers may surprise you. The least that can happen is that you are able to dissociate and distance yourself from your partner's attitudes and feelings. This distance can allow you to be more objective and to differentiate between your feelings and those of your partner's.

Assume Major Responsibility

When you have an Exhibitionist destructive narcissistic partner, you may have to assume the major responsibility for the care and welfare of the family. Your partner will be too busy enhancing his image and too self-absorbed to give time and energy to caring for the family. He can be counted on for the grand gestures, but not for the day-to-day tasks.

Your feelings about this are an important piece. You may think that it is only right and proper that you assume these responsibilities, as your partner has more important things to do. You may be resigned or resentful of the imbalance. However, your feelings can impact the quality of your family's life and your self-esteem. You may want to reflect on your feelings and their impact on the family.

If you are having to assume major responsibility, there may be no other solution. Your partner is unlikely to change, to become empathic, and to begin to actively participate. Nor will your partner understand any other way of behaving. Try not to waste your time being resentful or angry. That will not make any difference to your partner, and may have a negative impact on the rest of the family and the quality of their lives. This is another instance where the best you may be able to do is to grin and bear it.

Make Excuses

Are you prone to making excuses for your partner's lack of sensitivity? Do you become embarrassed when they do or say something that hurts, rejects, or devalues another person (for example, your children, family members, friends, acquaintances, or strangers)? Do you try to soothe over these situations by giving reasons for the insensitivity? Reasons that try to put the behavior in a better light? Do you believe your excuses?

If you are doing any of these, then you are taking on responsibility for your partner's behaviors and attitudes, and failing to understand your limits and boundaries. You may want to explore why it is important to you to have others think well of your partner. Are you under the impression that how others perceive your partner reflects on how they perceive you? Certainly some of that may be true, but the important point is that you feel that your partner is hurting other people, being unkind, thoughtless, and insensitive, and that you have the responsibility to fix it. This belief can keep you very busy, cleaning up after your partner.

Your best strategy will be to stop making these excuses. Instead of making excuses, you can repair the empathic failure of your partner, or at least try to repair it. Insensitivity or thoughtlessness are empathic failures. Your partner ignored the other person's feelings. What could be effective is for you to respond to the person as you think or feel an empathic person would; that is, do the opposite of what your partner does. For example, if your partner makes a caustic remark about someone's weight, and you saw that it bothered the person, you could find something positive about the person and comment on that. Anything would work, such as, "I've always thought you have pretty eyes," or "That is a good color for you," or "I like how your hair is styled." Try to get out of the practice of saying things like, "My partner didn't mean to hurt your feelings," or other excuses. You are not responsible for what your partner does or says. Making excuses just supports this behavior.

Status Conscious

How status conscious are you? Do you feel you should only associate with people you consider as social equals or as superior? Do you examine what these people are doing, saying, and possessing and seek to emulate them? Do you have to belong to certain clubs, organizations, churches, or attend certain schools or events, because they fit with your perception of your status or desired status? Are you respectful, open, tolerant, and accepting of everyone, or just those you consider worthy? These and other indices of being status conscious may be encouraging and supportive of your Exhibitionist destructive narcissistic partner. These are likely to be some of his attitudes and behaviors, and if you tend to share them, then that validates his perceptions.

These are the behaviors and attitudes that convey a superior attitude, contempt for being different in any way, arrogance, and a devaluing of others. Yes, you will tend to associate with people that are similar to you in important ways, but that doesn't mean you have to be conscious of status or differences, or to think that others are inferior. Nor does it mean that you and your associates are the only people of value and importance. This attitude mirrors some of the more negative qualities of destructive narcissism.

If you are status conscious, you may want to examine what is at the root of your attitude and belief. This self-reflection can help you understand if old parental messages, your self-perception, or underdeveloped narcissism are playing roles in your attitude and behavior. You may be unconsciously accepting a value or belief that has not been examined and freely chosen. Or, you could feel that your self-esteem is bolstered with this reflected status. Or, you may have a perception that some others are inferior to you. Whatever your basic root cause may be, you can work to change it. You can become more personally secure by accepting, tolerating, and respecting a wider range of people and by reducing your need to be status conscious.

Chapter 9

Building Your Self

The previous eight chapters described people with different destructive narcissistic patterns, presented a guide for self-examination of some behaviors and attitudes that you may exhibit that are encouraging and supportive of your partner's DNP, and suggested strategies that can be used to help you protect yourself and better cope with your partner's troubling behaviors and attitudes and your triggered unpleasant feelings. The protective and coping strategies can be summarized as:

- giving up the fantasy that your partner will change,

- not trying to force or entice your partner to change,

- not confronting your partner to try and get your needs met or to change your partner,

- changing your expectations of yourself, your partner, and the relationship to make them realistic,

- employing your emotional insulation to ward off projections, projective identifications, and your personal triggered feelings,

- not trying to empathize, as this opens you up to projections and will not be reciprocated,

- withdrawing from the struggle, conflict, and battle of wills,

- finding someone you trust to confide in and vent to,

- building yourself strong and resilient boundaries,

- developing your personal healthy adult narcissism and reducing any aspect of underdeveloped narcissism that you may have, and

- cultivating resiliency.

Exercises in various chapters were presented to guide you to increased awareness of the feelings, fantasies, expectations, and assumptions that you have for yourself, your partner, and the relationship, and how to implement strategies, such as emotional insulation.

We now turn to explaining how to begin to build your strong and resilient boundaries, reduce underdeveloped narcissism in and for yourself, and cultivate resiliency. What is presented here is intended to kick start your thinking about yourself and what you can do that will prevent, reduce, and eliminate some of the distressing feelings you have in response to your partner's behavior and attitudes, allow your self-esteem and self-confidence to be firm and not become eroded, and help you think of positive and constructive responses to your partner. These are only a beginning.

Underdeveloped Narcissism

You may have some aspects of yourself that reflect underdeveloped narcissism, although these may not reach the level and extent to be categorized as a destructive narcissistic pattern. Even if you have a few of these, you can work to increase your healthy adult narcissism, which is defined here as:

- being appropriately empathic,

- having a wide range of emotional expression,

- focusing less on self-absorption and more on having concern and caring for others,

- having a self-care and self-focus that preserve your integrity,

- having an understanding of self as separate and distinct from others,

- having a realistic sense of responsibility,

- being creative,

- having an appropriate sense of humor, and

- having a willingness to be self-examining, self-reflective, and self-corrective.

You probably have some sense of the personal work on underdeveloped narcissism that needs to be done after reading the first eight chapters in this book. You may have seen some of your behaviors, attitudes, feelings, and perspectives in the descriptions for the DNP in the various categories. But it is most likely that you did not see this, because one characteristic of those with underdeveloped narcissism, both those with a DNP and those without, is the inability to see their underdeveloped narcissism. We all share that inability. You cannot see where you lack appropriate separation and individuation, and have deficits in psychological growth and development. Nor can you understand at this point what you are doing, saying, or believing that is troubling others. You simply cannot see it.

Let's accept that you have some aspects of underdeveloped narcissism and that you are unaware of it. Since you cannot identify what is underdeveloped, it becomes difficult to work on constructive changes. What can be helpful for you at this point is to accept these two points as your working hypotheses: first you have underdeveloped narcissism, and second you remain unaware of it. We are not going to spend time trying to identify what aspects of underdeveloped narcissism you have, nor are we trying to fix it. That is beyond the scope of this book.

What can be done is to introduce you to ways in which you can build some healthy adult narcissism and encourage you to work through the exercises in this chapter with that goal in mind. The reasoning behind this approach is that when you build your healthy adult narcissism, you become more aware of your underdeveloped narcissism, and you reduce or eliminate some of the feelings, attitudes, and behaviors that are supportive of underdeveloped narcissism.

The exercises and discussions here will focus on three aspects for development.

1. Increasing your range and depth of emotional experience and expression.

2. Identifying the difference between self-absorption and an appropriate self-focus, as in self-care.

3. Becoming more realistically empathic.

These are only three of the many aspects of narcissism.

Increase Emotional Range and Depth

The person with healthy adult narcissism has a wide range of emotions, both felt and expressed. These emotions are also deep, and not shallow. If you were to characterize your emotions as the heart of yourself, or your being, you get some sense of just how important having a range and depth of feeling and expression can be. Building yourself in this way allows you to connect with others in more meaningful ways, communicate more clearly, and increase your understanding of others.

A restricted range of emotions and shallow emotions limit connections to others and understanding of self and others. What generally happens in these circumstances is that the emotions that are felt or expressed tend to be primitive, intense, and negative. By primitive we mean that they are the first emotions experienced by the infant, which are continuing to be experienced by the person in much the same way as they were earlier in life. For example, anger is experienced as an all-consuming rage, much like the infant's anger. These emotions also tend to be intense. That is, the person does not experience milder forms of feelings, such as irritation instead of anger. In addition to the two previous characteristics, the emotions tend to be negative. These people seldom, if ever, experience true happiness, joy, or other positive emotions. They may have the words, but don't have the feelings behind the words. These are all good reasons for increasing the range and depth of your emotional experiencing and expression. Following are some exercises to get you started.

Awareness Exercise 1: Mild Feelings

Objectives: To help you to focus on mild feelings, become aware of the associated sensations, and increase your awareness of how and when to express these mild feelings.

Materials: Stiff paper such as memory book paper available from crafts stores, glue stick, a variety of catalogues and magazines from which to cut pictures, a set of colored felt tip markers, a pen, and writing paper.

Directions:

1. For each of the following six mild feelings, you are invited to draw a picture, construct a collage, compose a poem, or

write an essay. Each exercise focuses on a different mild feeling. It could be helpful to look up the definition in the dictionary, think about it, and see what it feels like to you.

2. After completing your product, sit in silence and reflect on the feeling and your bodily sensations. Write a brief description of the feeling on the back of your product.

- Irritation

- Delight

- Apprehension

- Affection

- Embarrassment

- Melancholy

Reflection: After you complete all or most of these, review what you produced and described. Resolve to tune in to see if you are experiencing any of these at least once a day for a week. Try to become more aware of these milder feelings.

Awareness Exercise 2:
Milder Positive Feelings

Objectives: To become more comfortable verbalizing your milder emotions and learn new ways to express what you are experiencing in the moment.

Materials: Paper, a pen, and a calendar.

Directions: Find a place where you can sit and write, free from distractions and interruptions. Plan to allow at least thirty minutes for this activity.

1. Sit in silence and reflect on what you became aware of when experiencing delight from the previous exercise. Allow yourself to feel some of the bodily sensations you have when you are delighted.

2. As you are reflecting, some people, things, situations, and events may come to mind as examples of delight for you. Make a list of these and continuously try to expand your list with other examples.

Examples:

- Did you tell someone you were glad (or delighted) to see them, or express something positive about that person?

- Did you comment about your delight at viewing something? (For example, an unexpected field of wildflowers.)

- Did you say thank you to a child for doing something for you, or for doing something that was delightful?

3. Review your list and place a check mark (✓) by those where you openly, authentically, and directly expressed your delight at that moment. Don't use nominal gestures, such as smiling, to substitute for verbal expression.

4. Review your list once again and become aware of the missed opportunities for expression of your feelings.

5. Make a resolution to increase open expressions of your delight and put a cross mark (x) on the calendar each day that you accomplish this. There are many sources of delight and many ways to express it.

6. Once you complete steps 1–5, do the same for the terms affection and melancholy.

Milder Negative Feelings

It can be more difficult to begin to express mild negative feelings, such as irritation. And it may not be appropriate, helpful, or constructive to do so at many times, or with some people. Actually, since your destructive narcissistic partner doesn't really care about your feelings, you may be better off not expressing your negative feelings to them. However, you can expand your range and depth of feeling and expression with others, making it less important to be able to say them to your partner. You have other outlets.

You may be in the habit of suppressing mild negative feelings, on the assumption that they are not important, or that only intense feelings are important and need to be expressed. This stance has some validity, as you do not need to express every negative feeling you have. On the other hand, when you suppress, repress, or deny milder feelings, they can build up and become more intense ones. For example, when you do not express your irritation, you can continue to be irritated by events or people, until that irritation intensifies to anger. The more intense feelings have a negative effect on your physical health, your psychological health, and on your relationships.

There is the possibility that you really are not aware when you feel mild versions of feelings, such as apprehension or irritation. It's not that you don't have these feelings, it is that you are blocking your awareness of them. Blocking your awareness of these feelings over a period of time and not having the strategies to work through or resolve them can lead to physical health concerns, such as high blood pressure, stomach and digestive upsets, and headaches. Emotional disruptions can also lead to psychological concerns, such as depression, rapid mood changes, and inappropriate outbursts. There are numerous beneficial reasons for learning to become aware of your milder negative feelings.

We'll focus on four milder versions for some common negative feelings. There are several levels for each of these, such as those presented in the following table. These are presented from mild to intense. Thus, irritation is the milder form of rage; disquiet is the milder form of terror; feeling blamed or blame-worthy is the milder form of guilt; and embarrassment is the milder form of shame. You probably have little difficulty in being aware when you are experiencing the strong and intense versions, but you also can increase your awareness of feeling the milder ones.

Table 1: Levels for Four Negative Feelings

Levels	Feelings			
	Anger	Fear	Guilt	Shame
Mildest	Irritation	Disquiet	Blamed	Embarrass-ment
	Displeasure	Apprehen-sion	At fault	Unworthy
	Annoyance	Alarm	Remorseful	Disgraceful
Strong	Anger	Dread	Guilt	Indecent
	Fury	Fear	Condem-nation	Humiliation

Intensive	Rage	Terror	Repre-hensible	Shame

Awareness Exercise 3: Mild Versions

Objectives: To increase your awareness of what sensations mild feelings have for you, focus on your meanings for these versions, and explore how you can enhance your awareness of the feelings.

Materials: Four sheets of drawing paper, such as newsprint, a set of felt markers or crayons, four sheets of writing paper, and a pen or pencil.

Directions: Work through each of the feelings one at a time; completely finish one before beginning the next.

1. Find a place where you can work undisturbed. This place should have adequate lighting, a table, and a comfortable chair.

2. Sit in silence and focus on the feeling with which you are working. When you are ready, use a sheet of your writing paper and list all words, phrases, associations, events, people, etc. that come to your mind as you reflect on the feeling. Try to list eight to ten of these.

3. Review your list. Use a different color for each of the items and draw a shape, symbol, splotch of color, or whatever you desire that illustrates that item for you.

- Irritation
- Disquiet or concern
- At fault
- Embarrassed

Reflection: After completing step 3 for embarrassed, review your lists and products. Try to capture what these milder versions of feelings feel like for you and fix them in your mind. Resolve to frequently tune in to what you are experiencing and to check to see if you feel any of the milder versions. You can then take steps to express the feelings, or to evaluate and analyze what is causing you to feel as you do. Expressing the feeling is venting; it's mild, so your expression is managed and contained, and it is unlikely that someone else will get upset.

It could be helpful for you to analyze and evaluate the causes for your feelings. There are basic causes for each of the categories, such as anger, and you can sort through what is happening, internally and externally, to produce these feelings for you. The basic causes tend to be:

A threat to your existence and welfare	Anger
The possibility of destruction or danger	Fear
Failure to live up to personal, moral, and ethical standards	Guilt
A fear that your essential self is flawed	Shame

So when you feel irritated, you'll want to assess what is perceived as a threat and how much of a threat it is. When you feel a sense of disquiet, you will want to examine where you are becoming aware of danger or possible danger. When you feel at fault for something, you will need to assess the extent of your responsibility. And when you feel embarrassed, you will want to assess if you made a mistake and can forgive yourself, or if you need to feel you are fatally flawed.

Expand Emotions

The final exercise and discussion focuses on expanding your feeling vocabulary and expression. You probably think and use few feeling words. It can be helpful to expand your vocabulary, as well as become more precise about what you are experiencing. The following exercise will take some time and effort to complete but at the conclusion you will have many more words and phrases to express more precisely what you are experiencing.

Expression Exercise 4: Feeling Vocabulary

Objectives: To expand the number of words you know and use to express your feelings and provide you with a resource to consult when you have difficulty thinking of words to express your feelings.

Materials: Loose-leaf notebook, stiff paper, such as memory book paper available from craft stores, hole puncher, glue, set of felt markers or crayons, paper and pen, and a variety of magazines and catalogues from which to cut pictures.

Procedure: The material will be used to construct a Book of Feelings. Each page will either be a collage, drawing, poem, or essay.

Activities:

- **Collage:** Select pictures, words, and symbols from the magazines and catalogues that describe the designated concept. Cut these out and glue them to a sheet of the stiff paper. If you have a selection of colored paper, select the color that relates to the concept in some way for you. Write the title of the concept at the top of the page. Arrange the cut pictures on the page prior to gluing them. Use any arrangement you choose.

- **Drawing:** Drawings can be realistic, symbolic, abstract, or nonobjective. You don't have to have a drawing talent to create a picture. Use the felt markers or crayons to draw the images that emerge for you as you reflect on the designated concept.

- **Poem:** Poems do not have to follow any predetermined form for this activity. Poems are used here to express the thoughts, ideas, and feelings that emerge as you ponder the designated concept. Just write whatever comes up for you.

- **Essay:** This could be a story, essay, or description where you write about a designated concept. Don't worry about technical matters, as this Book is for you. It will be easier for you to write if you just concentrate on expressing your thoughts, ideas, and feelings.

Directions: Following is a list of feeling words. First, look up the definitions in a dictionary or a thesaurus. Next, think about what images, symbols, activities, or events seem to be connected to the defined word in some way. Finally, use any two of the described activities above to create one to three pages in your book about the feeling. Construct one to three pages about each word.

uncertain	hurt	proud	betrayed	ineffective
excited	envious	curious	serene	appreciative
alienated	pleased	devalued	energized	

Differentiating between Self-Absorption and Self-Focus

Because you cannot see your personal undeveloped narcissism, you may not be aware of what you are doing and saying that is reflective of that underdevelopment. It is much easier to see others' self-absorption than it is to be aware of your own. Compounding the difficulty can be the need and responsibility to take care of yourself. Understanding the difference between appropriate self-care and self-focus and being self-absorbed is not always easy to do.

Can you distinguish between the following?

- Wondering what someone thinks of you versus needing to have someone like you.

- Concern about quality of your performance versus having to be perfect.

- Wanting something versus demanding that you be given what you want.

- Accepting responsibility for your feelings versus thinking that others are causing or making you feel as you do.

- Doing something for someone because you want to versus doing something because someone else wants you to do whatever it is.

- Being assertive versus being aggressive or passive.

These are but a few of the ways that self-focus (the former) differs from the self-absorption (the latter).

Self-focus means that you:

- understand where you end and where others begin,

- maintain strong and resilient psychological boundaries,

- ask for what you want and need, but do not demand that you receive it,

- are appreciative of being recognized and respected, but not resentful or angry when you are not,

- don't demand that others conform to your expectation,

- do not allow yourself to be exploited or manipulated,

- allow others to have and express their feelings,

- can access your feelings and express them in appropriate ways,

- have reasonable and realistic expectations of yourself,

- accept and act to take care of your needs without dismissing or trampling others' rights, and

- are self-reflective and self-examining.

In order to know whether you are self-absorbed rather than having a self-focus, you have to be willing to consider that you do have some attitudes and behaviors that are reflective of some aspects of underdeveloped narcissism. You don't have to dwell on these or be ashamed, you just have to recognize these and work to change them. Changing is also a process that takes time, effort, and attention. It will not be easy to continually ask yourself the hard questions and to be constantly alert to your self-absorbed behaviors and attitudes. But it can be done.

Another possibility for determining your areas of personal undeveloped narcissism is to examine those aspects you have in common with your partner, or the ones for which you make excuses, rationalize, or ignore in your partner. These shared behaviors and attitudes are likely to be overlooked by you because, of course, you cannot see them. Suspend your disbelief and judgmental stance briefly, and complete the next exercise.

Identification Exercise 5:
Personal Underdeveloped Narcissism

Objectives: To explore and identify possible areas of personal underdeveloped narcissism.

Materials: A sheet of paper and a pen.

Directions: Find a quiet place where you can work free from distractions for about thirty minutes. Read the list of behaviors and attitudes and place a check mark beside each one that is descriptive of your partner in the column titled, "Your Partner." Next, place a check mark beside each behavior and attitude that fits you, or for which you are criticized. Review what you checked to determine how you and your partner are similar in behavior and attitudes. These can be the areas where you are collaborating with you partner in their destructive narcissism.

Finally, review the items you checked for yourself. These are the possible areas of your underdeveloped narcissism. They can form a list of things you can work to change. This is the beginning of your action plan for positive changes. Review the previous chapters in this book, read the specific descriptions for behaviors and attitudes reflective of the areas you checked, and make a list of specific actions you can take.

Behaviors and Attitudes	Your Partner	Yourself
Attention seeking		
Yearns for admiration		
Excitement attitude		
Shallow emotions		
Lack of empathy		
Exploits others		
Boasts and brags		
Sense of superiority		
Emptiness		
Easily irritated or angered		
Takes unearned credit		
Quickly switches from poor me state to inflated state		
Envious		
Jealous		
Cannot delay gratification		
Acts recklessly or takes unnecessary risks		
Tries to manipulate and control		
Lies and makes misleading statements		
Contemptuous		
Demeans and devalues others		

Become More Realistically Empathic

In my book, *Whose Life Is It Anyway?*, the focus is on "when to stop taking care of their feelings and take care of your own." This book is a guide to developing strong and resilient boundaries, and is about how to be appropriately empathic. The premise of the book is that lack of boundary strength can lead to your becoming overwhelmed, enmeshed, or engulfed by others' feelings, and that you are diagnosing this as being overly empathic. In reality, you are catching and acting on others' feelings, without being able to protect yourself from catching and identifying with the other person's feeling and losing your sense of self in the process. This is not empathy. When you are empathic, you do not lose your sense of self; you sense, but do not catch, what the other person is feeling. You do not identify with the other person's feelings; you cannot be unconsciously manipulated, nor do you remain trapped or mixed in with the other person's intensity. These are characteristics for appropriate and realistic empathy.

On the other hand, you are not appropriately and realistically empathic, if you feel that:

- you frequently become lost in your partner's feelings,

- you are caught and manipulated by your partner's feelings,

- you tend to be overwhelmed, enmeshed, and engulfed by your partner's feelings,

- you cannot pull back from your partner's intense feelings at will,

- you remain connected to their intense feelings, long after the interaction ceases,

- you agree to do things you do not want to do, or

- you feel that you are overly empathic with your partner and others.

What is more likely is that you lack sufficient psychological boundary strength and resilience.

Another aspect of appropriate and realistic empathy is that you do not want to stop being empathic for fear of any of the above happening. You can always use your emotional insulation to prevent catching others' emotions. That does work. However, you don't want to insulate yourself so well that you are never empathic or seldom empathic. That stance will cut you off from meaningful connections that you will want to preserve.

The tasks are to protect yourself from being caught and acting on others' emotions and to build your psychological boundary strength, so that it is strong and resilient. You do not want to have boundaries that are rigid or soft, as these will not allow you to have realistic and appropriate empathy.

Healthy adult narcissism has empathy as one of its main characteristics, and this is your goal. Developing strong and resilient boundaries is a major component of empathy, and you can work to develop yours. Seek assistance from a mental health professional, become self-reflective, read books on the subject, such as the one mentioned previously, and practice the exercises in this book to achieve your goal. This is long term, as your psychological boundaries were not appropriately developed earlier. It will take time and effort to overcome these deficits. It can be done, but you must be patient with yourself and continue to work on it. In the interim, here are some helpful, intermediate strategies that you can implement.

- Remind yourself to use your emotional insulation with your partner.

- When intense negative emotions start to emerge within you, stop and think about putting your emotional insulation in place.

- Use self-talk to remind yourself to allow others to assume responsibility for their feelings, and that you don't have to make them feel better.

- Practice being assertive.

These are some techniques for fortifying your boundaries that can help protect you in many interactions. They will not be full protection, because you cannot or will not want to keep your guard up with your partner. Keeping a wall between you and your partner will not help the relationship. It's impossible to have any guidelines for when to employ these techniques, and when not to use them with your partner. They keep the other person at a distance, and this is not considered to be constructive for an intimate relationship. You will have to make the decision about if, when, and how to use these strategies.

There is one additional strategy that can both help in inter-actions with your destructive narcissistic partner and build your appropriate and realistic empathy skills. You can begin to use what was previously described as "active listening and responding," where you attend to the speaker, and identify and respond to their feelings without actually feeling what the speaker is feeling. This strategy has the effect of:

- letting the other person know that they were heard and understood,

- keeping you detached and disassociated from their emotions,

- preventing you from catching their emotions, and

- moderating the possibility of having your feelings trig-gered, while reaching out and connecting with that person.

You can make empathic responses without being empathic with this strategy.

Active listening and responding means that you pay attention to the speaker and try to discern what the real message is, because the content or words seldom convey the real message. That real message is the meta-communication, which forms over 90 percent of the message, while content forms less than 10 percent of the message. Part of your reason for catching others' emotions could be that you are very open to the meta-communication without realiz-ing it, and you respond to that message and not the actual content. The primary components for meta-communication are:

- feelings,

- intent or motivation,

- needs, wishes, desires,

- fantasies, and/or

- projections and transferences.

That is, the speaker is presenting some or all of these, but they are not open, direct, specific, or even known consciously by the speaker. You will not understand all of these, even for yourself, but you can learn to be aware and "read" some of these. In order to read, you have to remain primarily on the thinking level, and not the feeling level.

I will begin with a personal example of meta-communication. One Friday evening, my fifteen-year-old son said that he was going over to a friend's house. I asked him what time he was going to come home, and he said, "One o'clock." I said that was too late. He looked at me and said, "Mother, if you have a time you want me home, just tell me." I said, "Eleven o'clock." And he said, "Okay." He was actually home by ten o'clock. It is an example of "reading" a meta-communication. He read my feelings, and my intent and wish were communicated to him. He understood that I do have an upper limit on what I consider to be an acceptable time frame, but had not directly said so.

Another example of meta-communication can be seen in the following interaction:

Speaker: Did you remember to pick up the clothes from the cleaners?

Receiver: No, I did not have time. I'll pick them up tomorrow.

Speaker: That's too late. You know that I need that suit for the meeting tomorrow. Why didn't you take the time? You never seem to be able to do what you need to do.

It will be difficult to tune in to the feelings, because this is written and we cannot see the nonverbal gesture, but we can guess at some feelings that the speaker may have, for example, irritation, frustration, and apprehension. The speaker is also blaming and critical. We're not able to judge the validity of their comments and, although that could be important, it isn't critical. An empathic response would require you to feel the same feelings as does the speaker. An active listening response would require that you acknowledge some or all of the speaker's feelings. One active listening response could be:

Receiver: You are irritated that I wasn't able to pick up your suit and frustrated that I didn't seem to realize how important this was for you.

The receiver could stop at this point or go on to explain or apologize, if that is really warranted. Many receivers would respond to the speaker's last two statements that are blaming and critical and become defensive or attacking. These statements can be really hurtful, and a tendency could be to focus on them, rather than the first two statements that carry much of the importance of the message. The blaming and criticizing are the outgrowth of the annoyance and frustration, probably present for the first two statements. Once your emotions get triggered, for example, by blame and criticism, you start responding based on their influence, which turns the exchange into a self-protective stance for both of you. That is not a constructive stance.

An active listening response has several components: attention to the content and feelings; a reading of the nonverbal communication, such as gesture and voice tone; emotional insulation of personal feelings; a thinking stance for the receiver; and responding to the meta-communication of the speaker. All of these are important, but responding to the meta-communication is critical.

It can be a big jump for you to start giving active listening responses. You may also find it hard to keep a thinking focus, and you may have to consciously remind yourself to think. One positive outcome of this response is that you may be less churned up, upset, or emotionally intense by using active listening and responding. You are still giving the speaker your attention, focusing on them and at the same time remaining somewhat remote and detached. You can practice giving these responses in the following exercise.

Active Listening Exercise 6:
Thinking Responses

Objective: To practice active listening and responding.

Materials: A sheet of paper and a pen or a pencil.

Directions: Assume you are the receiver in each of the following scenes.

1. Identify some possible feelings that the speaker may be experiencing.

2. Use that information to formulate a response. You can think of the speaker as your destructive narcissistic partner, or you can imagine someone else.

- *Speaker:* You are wonderful, and I want to get to know you better.

    Possible feelings:

    Response:

- *Speaker:* Don't you want to make me proud of you?

  Possible feelings:

  Response:

- *Speaker:* It seems to me that if you cared about me, you'd want to please me.

  Possible feelings:

  Response:

- *Speaker:* Just once, I wish you could get something right.

  Possible feelings:

  Response:

Review your responses. Do they identify a possible feeling for the speaker? Are your responses free from your personal concerns and feelings? Did you try to explain, excuse, rationalize, or do anything that could be defensive on your part? Not having access to the nonverbal behavior that accompanied the verbal response is limiting, but you can still make guesses and try to formulate a thinking response.

Summary

You now have some information, self-knowledge, understanding, and strategies that can help you cope with your narcissistic partner, who may have a destructive narcissistic pattern, or who has considerable underdeveloped narcissism. These are some important points to remember.

- This person is unaware of the impact of their behavior on you and others.

- You cannot do or say anything that will cause your partner to become more aware or to change.

- You may unconsciously be supportive of some behaviors and attitudes, or you may be similar to your partner in many ways.

- You cannot see your personal underdeveloped narcissism, just as your partner cannot see theirs.

- There are strategies to help you. One important one is emotional insulation, which can help you by blocking unconscious projections from others and teaching you how to cope with your triggered feelings.

- Working to develop your healthy adult narcissism will be more rewarding than trying to change your partner, or staying mired in misery.

References

Berube, M. (ed.) 1999. *Webster's II New College Dictionary.* Boston Mass.: Houghton-Mifflin.

Brown, N. 1998. *The Destructive Narcissistic Pattern.* Westport, Conn.: Praeger.

Brown, N. 2002. *Children of the Self-Absorbed: A Grownup's Guide to Getting Over Narcissistic Parents.* Oakland, Calif.: New Harbinger Publications.

Brown, N. 2002. *Whose Life Is It Anyway? When to Stop Taking Care of Their Feelings and Start Taking Care of Your Own.* Oakland, Calif.: New Harbinger Publications.

Hatfield, E., J. T. Cacioppo, and R. L. Rapson. 1994. *Emotional Contagion.* Cambridge, United Kingdom: Cambridge University Press.

Mahler, M., and M. Furer. 1968. *On Human Symbiosis and the Vicissitudes of Individuation: Infantile Psychoses.* New York: International Universities Press.

Some Other
New Harbinger Titles

Helping A Child with Nonverbal Learning Disorder, 2nd edition
  Item 5266 $15.95
The Introvert & Extrovert in Love, Item 4863 $14.95
Helping Your Socially Vulnerable Child, Item 4580 $15.95
Life Planning for Adults with Developmental Disabilities, Item 4511 $19.95
But I Didn't Mean That! Item 4887 $14.95
The Family Intervention Guide to Mental Illness, Item 5068 $17.95
It's So Hard to Love You, Item 4962 $14.95
The Turbulent Twenties, Item 4216 $14.95
The Balanced Mom, Item 4534 $14.95
Helping Your Child Overcome Separation Anxiety & School Refusal,
  Item 4313 $14.95
When Your Child Is Cutting, Item 4375 $15.95
Helping Your Child with Selective Mutism, Item 416X $14.95
Sun Protection for Life, Item 4194 $11.95
Helping Your Child with Autism Spectrum Disorder, Item 3848 $17.95
Teach Me to Say It Right, Item 4038 $13.95
Grieving Mindfully, Item 4011 $14.95
The Courage to Trust, Item 3805 $14.95
The Gift of ADHD, Item 3899 $14.95
The Power of Two Workbook, Item 3341 $19.95
Adult Children of Divorce, Item 3368 $14.95
Fifty Great Tips, Tricks, and Techniques to Connect
with Your Teen, Item 3597 $10.95
Helping Your Child with OCD, Item 3325 $19.95
Helping Your Depressed Child, Item 3228 $14.95

Call **toll free, 1-800-748-6273,** or log on to our online bookstore at **www.newharbinger.com** to order. Have your Visa or Mastercard number ready. Or send a check for the titles you want to New Harbinger Publications, Inc., 5674 Shattuck Ave., Oakland, CA 94609. Include $4.50 for the first book and 75¢ for each additional book, to cover shipping and handling. (California residents please include appropriate sales tax.) Allow two to five weeks for delivery.

Prices subject to change without notice.